DREAMLAND

DREAMLAND
The Way Out of Juárez

WORDS BY CHARLES BOWDEN

DRAWINGS BY ALICE LEORA BRIGGS

University of Texas Press
Austin

For Bill Conroy of narconews.com, who stood his watch when others
turned away and pretended none of this had happened.

C.B.

For Pedro. He knows why.

A.L.B.

For Kelly Leslie, who cooked up Dreamland
from the raw stuff we brought home.

C.B. and A.L.B.

Requests for permission to reproduce material
from this work should be sent to:
    Permissions
    University of Texas Press
    P.O. Box 7819
    Austin, TX 78713-7819
    www.utexas.edu/utpress/about/bpermission.html

∞ The paper used in this book meets the minimum
requirements of ANSI/NISO Z39.48-1992 (R1997)
(Permanence of Paper).

Library of Congress Cataloging-in-Publication Data

Bowden, Charles, 1945–
Dreamland : [the way out of Juárez] / words by Charles Bowden ; drawings by Alice Leora Briggs. — 1st ed.
    p.   cm.
  ISBN 978-0-292-72123-4 (cloth : alk. paper) — ISBN 978-0-292-72207-1 (pbk. : alk. paper)
   1. Drug traffic—Mexico—Ciudad Juárez. 2. Narco-terrorism—Mexico—Ciudad Juárez. 3. Ciudad Juárez
(Mexico)—Social conditions. I. Briggs, Alice Leora, 1953– II. Title.
  HV5840.M42C5825 2010
  363.450972'16—dc22

2009046117

Each slow turn of the world carries such disinherited ones to whom neither the past nor the future belongs. For even the immediate future is far from mankind. This shouldn't confuse us; no, it should commit us to preserve the form we still can recognize. This stood among men, once, stood in the middle of fate, the annihilator, stood in the middle of Not-Knowing-Where-To, as if it existed, and it pulled down stars from the safe heaven toward it.

Rainer Maria Rilke,
Duino Elegies

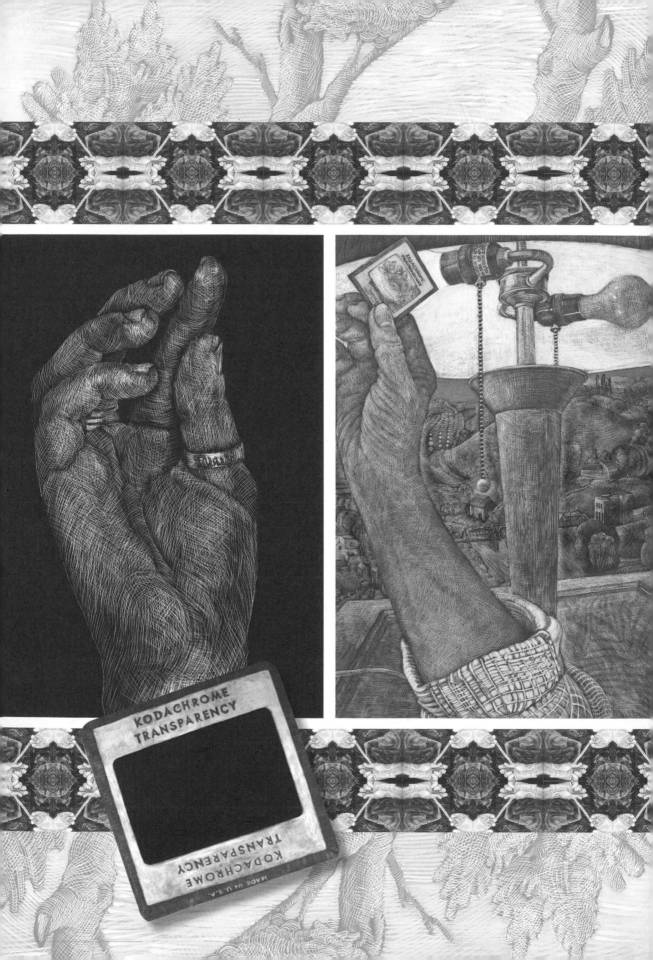

he room was painted a very light green and the blinds were shut. The air felt stale and fear rolled off the man's body. He turned on a lamp and held a color slide to the light: a black hand reached out of the sand dune just beyond the city. Of course, I knew about bodies coming out of the sand, often with money in their mouths. Everyone knew about the bodies.

Still, that black hand gave me pause.

The photographer believed it was deliberately left reaching out of the dune, left to beckon the curious and the ignorant and the idle to a new kind of reality.

I bought the slide from him and carried it with me a long time. I would take it out and hold it to the light, sometimes in a lonely room on the road, sometimes to the morning sun as steam rose off my coffee. This was before the woman was found in the barrel of acid or the many other events.

I think that is when it began for me, in that apartment with light green walls, the blinds shut, and the slide glowing over the bulb in the lamp. A hand reaching out to heaven from the sands.

It took eight or ten years for me to understand that moment. I sensed at the time some kind of mooring slipping free in my life. But this feeling was fleeting and easily controlled. I told myself the hand in the dune, like the other bodies in the sand, like the woman in the barrel, that all these things were aberrations and that normal life continued undisturbed and as certain as dawn and as sound as money.

It took me time to realize the error of my ways.

You must forgive this failure to grasp reality. You see, I've always been a believer. I have always sought order and calm. I thought that was the way of the world. In the beginning I even thought the world kept getting better, the cars larger, and summer was girls in scanty clothes.

Two things stun me: how much I once believed and how much, despite the storm in the skies and the blood on the ground, that I still continue to believe.

There is a way out of here and it is called *levantón*, the lift or the pickup. You are going about your business and suddenly men with guns come and you go with them. Sometimes you return as a corpse, and this, of course, is a blessing since then your family knows your fate and can visit your grave. But usually you never come back in any form and so you become, not even a ghost, but a question mark.

The son of a professor in the city taught firearms to the state judicial police. He also had been an officer in the army. Then he vanished into the night and that is all that is known.

The State at times moves to respond to this reality. They create a new police unit, Grupo Zeus. The *levantón*s continue. The people vanish all along the line. No one has real numbers because people are afraid to report such disappearances to the police. This is wise. When the Federal police were dispatched to Nuevo Laredo, for example, the number of people disappearing zoomed. But then, this is the custom.

Los Zetas, also, are dreaded along the line. They are a product of the nation to the north—trained by the U.S. Army's Airmobile Special Forces Group in the fabled School of the Americas in Fort Benning, Georgia. They tired of this task and so joined a cartel.

Power can be identified here, also authority. But everything gets blurry when the standard of law and order is applied.

There are reports that struggle to put this frolic into perspective. Just as 150 people perished in Chiapas during the 1994 Zapatista uprising, and 3,348 died in around thirty years in Northern Ireland during the Troubles, one little state, Sinaloa, had 16,000 murders in about twenty years. So we can tally numbers and cluck over the level of mayhem. But something else is going on besides carnage. A Federal attorney for the nation to the south finally notes the obvious: the power of the drug industry has exceeded the power of the State. Men now operate outside the bounds of government and they are armed with bazookas and assault rifles. There is talk of ground-to-air missiles, also. Chihuahua creates a special anti-kidnapping force of eight skilled men—six are murdered, one vanishes.[1]

Presidents come and go and pretend to be in charge. Police officers also come and go. In one three-month period, seventy-eight

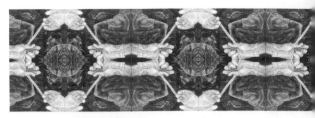

cops in the nation are slaughtered by drug merchants. Severed heads appear in municipal plazas. Bodies become messages with little written notes—"Is this how you protect your informants?"—and fingerless bodies show up near television stations, outside of military bases, or are plopped by the homes of big politicians. From time to time, the State announces that the drug merchants are on the run or being taken down. Then a video is mailed showing one group executing six members by what is believed to be members of the Federal police. In time, slaughters are posted on the Internet.

It becomes a blur, and yet, somehow I continue to believe, even though I know my beliefs are foolish and outdated.

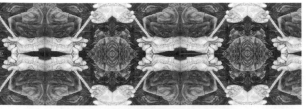

The heat is on. A mile or so away, the other nation stands in the same white light and dust. Blue sheen of wood smoke coats the air in winter. Brown waves of dirt color the air in summer. Sometimes the two cities vanish into clouds of dust but no one comments on this fact, nor on the cough that trails many residents down the street. The river divides them but now the river is a concrete ditch and sometimes the water is there and sometimes the water is absent. Everything is under control. Everything is planned or will be planned. There are laws, regulations, plans, treaties, economic targets, agencies, military personnel, electronic sensors, telephone intercepts, snitches, killers, thieves. Meetings. Twice as many of everything as normal because here two nations grind up against each other and two cities merge and a river runs between but then the river hardly ever runs anymore.

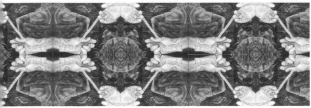

One city is called El Paso, the other Juárez. One state is called Texas, the other Chihuahua. One nation is called the United States, the other Mexico. I find it harder and harder to use these names because they imply order and boundaries, and both are breaking down. So I stumble and try not to say these names even though they have meaning, at least some meaning, left, and they are right there on the maps and road signs. But they have the feel of the past, of dust and ruin and dead dreams. And so I say them at times, but often I struggle to find a way around these words because uttering them or writing them down contributes to a big lie and helps trap people in a dying world.

He wants justice, but with a few conditions. He must not be named. His agency must not be named. He must not be quoted. He cannot have a face, an age, or a habit. He must not really exist. Nor can he have a gender, he must simply be called a person—one more element in the disguise. But he stresses he wants justice.

The first time we met in a home and he talked about not talking. He was nervous and angry, the face never smiling, the eyes narrow, the body rigid, and the nails perfectly manicured. He believed, believed absolutely and without reservation, believed in laws and in regulations and in sound practices and in crimes and in punishment. Belief rolled off him like incense at a mass.

Then we met in a café where the plates clattered when they hit the Formica-topped tables and the light poured in from the south. Two miles away a heroin slum brooded right on the line. Rich aroma rose off my enchiladas and the salsa brought beads of sweat to my forehead. This time he spoke more freely, but still he held back and, of course, he insisted that everything be off the record.

Then, I come back a third time. Harsh light falls through the west window as he leans forward in his chair in the motel by a freeway. Here, he says, read this but do not write down any exact quotes. He is not used to talking about secret things. A friend describes him as a company man, not a whistleblower.

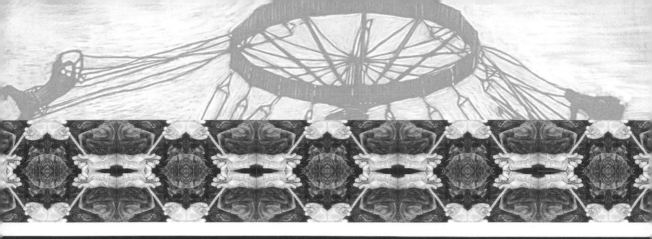

MEXICO

CANNABIS SATIVA

50 PESOS

CASA DE MONEDA DE LA NACION

UNITED STATES POSTAGE

08/05 2003

2 Fernando 2

CENTS

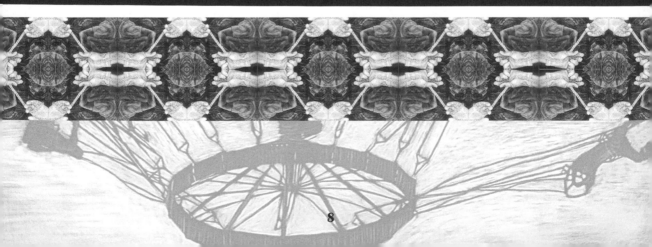

He soldiered on for the agency during the Central American wars, when everything sank into the murk of cocaine, Contras, the CIA, DEA, soldiers of fortune. And lies.

He believes and that is what people on the outside always miss, the passion and power of this belief. They join, they swear an oath and then slowly but surely they lose their illusions, sanction terrible things, watch crimes go unpunished in the name of national security or personal careers, endure and feel all these things, and yet they believe, believe despite the ugly facts, because they must believe or their lives mean nothing at all.

Five died, or twelve died, or fourteen died. He says it depends on who you count and when you begin the count.

In June, a DEA informant called Lalo was caught with about a hundred pounds of marijuana in a town in a nearby state, one only forty miles from this city. Juanita Fielding of the U.S. Attorney's office had the charges squashed because of an ongoing cigarette smuggling case by ICE (Immigration and Customs Enforcement) that employed Lalo as an informant. On August 5, Lalo tortured, killed, and buried a man in a condominium in the city on the other side of the river. By

January 14 the next year eleven more people went into the backyard of the condo, and at least one of them was an American resident alien. U.S. agencies knew Lalo was killing and did nothing lest they jeopardize the cigarette smuggling case. Or they knew of the killings and did nothing because they were trying to penetrate a cartel. The explanations varied as the dead came out of the ground. Then it blew up in their faces, and since then it has all been an effort to protect careers and deny responsibility.

So, he wants justice. He does not believe in the term "War on Drugs," not at all, because he sees the drug business as simply a law enforcement matter like burglary or shoplifting. Talk of war is overblown in his seasoned eyes. But law enforcement cannot sanction murder. He is firm on this point.

Besides, two men in his own agency, and their families, were almost brought to the

house of death by the informant who works for yet another agency. This is beyond the pale, he insists, this is intolerable.

I sit back and feel his waves of passion. He says when he was starting out he believed in a secret government as necessary and good. But now he does not. He thinks everything must be open. He sees the whole matter as an instance where government failed to function properly and this failure must be exposed and remedied.

He believes it is simply a matter of fixing the machinery, a slight adjustment and then all will be well.

I am drifting into a different way of seeing things. I want to say this: I think the death house is how government works on the line. The death house is remarkable only in that it became known. Few will agree with me, except for the dead. And they are gagged and kept out of sight by various headings: illegal immigration, illegal drugs, national security. The list keeps growing, as does the number of dead.

And I want to say that the house of death is not about death. The corpses are simply a by-product, like the duct tape used to gag the victims and the lime used to dissolve their bodies. The various agents involved, the various individuals, well, they are all about their own careers, about advancement and success in life. The dead are incidents in making federal cases or in moving loads of merchandise or in getting a little extra spending money for helping out at an execution.

But I always stall at this point, my tongue gets thick, words are difficult to utter. My mind races and yet speech ceases.

It is easier to see the whole house of corpses as a deviation from the natural order of things.

I try to form a single word that captures what I am seeing and feeling and thinking.

Finally, it comes out, to be sure it comes almost as a whisper. But still it comes.

Dreams.

He is still talking as the light slants through the window and dunes rise on the horizon. He is nicely dressed, good suit, necktie, shoes with a gloss. He takes pride in his appearance. He is an immigrant and his people fled communism and he believes in what he has found in this new land.

I make notes that will be off the record but

still be a record should the day ever come when he is willing to go public with his facts. I am at a kind of impasse of language—I can understand what he says but increasingly the words he uses mean nothing to me. An agency on this side knows of murders and does nothing. An agency on this side employs the killer and does nothing. An agency on the other side does the murders. A business that flourishes on both sides insists on the murders.

Eventually, he goes on the record and I see his name in newspapers and lawsuits and suddenly, there he is, Sandalio González, a man on fire against injustice and corruption. That is fine and I'm sure it helps. But, by then, I have moved on and I am past correcting problems. I have donned a smock and gone into a laboratory of dust and dirt and old clothing, a workroom equipped with a shovel and bones and gore.

I must find a new language, one that avoids empty words like justice and crime and punishment and problems and solutions.

A friend tells me a story to amuse me. He knows a girl and she runs a load across the line and she is arrested and does time in a prison on this side. When she is released,

she is fluent in English. But she cannot stand this side any longer and so she crosses back and hopes to put everything about her past behind her. She meets a man and they like each other very much. She can see a new life and he also sees a new life in her. And then she learns that he was the caretaker at yet another death house. This place I also know and can still feel the silence oozing out of the graves there. But no matter. She finally understands something: there is no escaping it, whatever it is. Because the language is failing everyone here. The business is illegal but the business employs police and Federal agents.

I can still say this side and that side. I can still say police and criminals. But the words are emptying out and the meaning is flowing down the *calles* and into the sewers.

The sewers, of course, are overloaded.

The name changes. Guillermo Ramírez Peyro is also known as Jesús Contreras, and also known as Eduardo, also known as Lalo. He was once a cop. Originally, he'd hoped to get a job working for the CIA but when that didn't pan out, he took what work came his way. He worked for Heriberto Santillán Tabares, an alleged captain in the local cartel. They both hired Miguel Loya Gallegos, the head of the night shift of the state police detachment in the city and a man with a relative high up in the Juárez cartel. Sometimes, he supplied other cops. Lalo also worked for DEA and then, when that failed, for ICE, a part of Homeland Security—for which he was paid at least $200,000.

From time to time, he surfaces and talks to courts or reporters. Then he vanishes once again into the catacombs of the American prison system.

His words catch the music of a new world that is being born.

On this occasion I went and bought a tarp to cover the floor. I bought eight bags of lime and went to pick up Alejandro Jr. Leaving him in charge of digging the hole and burying the bodies. The engineer Santillán asked me to have the house ready because he was going to have a *carne asada*, some "grilled meat". . .

CANAR

Serinus canarius

Reach for it, always reach for it, now snort or swallow or inject or light up or something, but for God's sakes reach for it, and don't ask what it is, no, no, no. Look in your purse or your wallet or your shirt pocket or your medicine chest. Or open up your heart and stare into the loneliness, train horn blowing after midnight and the bed is cold. The city lives under this appetite and on this appetite, lives because of the blues in faraway places, lives because of the after-hours lust in small towns and tired crossroads, lives on guns and death and money and nerves because the wide world craves an end to the emptiness and so the city never really sleeps but moves product or schemes product. Hundreds of gangs clog the lanes because of the hungers of people they will never meet but always service, and none of this is visible, no, and what is seen is the woman walking through the dust with a plastic bag of groceries in one hand and her ankles swollen and her face tired and still she trudges on and she is everywhere going about her errands, journeys never understood or noted but travels that fill the city with motion as the poor stagger along to get the few things they need, that roll of toilet paper, that bundle of diapers, the quart of milk, the stack of tortillas, the small bag of chiles and, of course, eggs and lard and the ankles are so thick and it is difficult to imagine those very ankles once held up a lithe young girl, a person now replaced by a tired face, an old sweater, sagging slacks and those thick ankles, swollen and yet never mentioned, not once mentioned in speech or newspapers or in any other media, a silence about the ankles and the aging women and the dust and those little plastic bags of items that are carried for miles and then put on an old table in a shack made of cardboard that sits in a dirt yard surrounded by pallets from loading docks.

Nor does anyone mention the black funnels of smoke from burning tires as the poor fire mud and dream of bricks.

The sewage trickling down the street while the young girls stroll by in hip-hugging pants, their small breasts teasing the stench in the air.

It is midnight or it is dawn or it is some other time and the hand reaches for the chemical compound that comes from this place and the bra unhooks, the panties fall, the music flows into the ears, the nose catches the scent of perfume, the eyes flicker and yearn

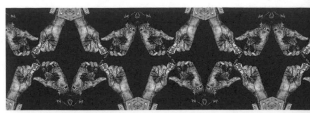

and everything comes from this place of dust and none of this is discussed and the hand rolls the paper and then strikes a match and the glow dances on the soft face and in the delight the sound of guns is muffled, the cord strangling the man goes unnoticed and the bags of lime ripped open to hasten the body on its way to rot, this, also, is unmentioned, everything it seems is unmentioned.

The world now is said to be global, and all the sounds and smells and all the deaths and loves are details in this fact.

Everything is normal now. And we keep track of this with numbers that comfort us in the twirl of events and the dust of our abandoned dreams. Or we ignore this with numbers that fill our heads and our accounting books.

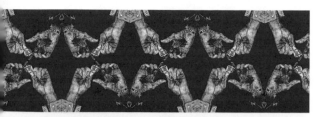

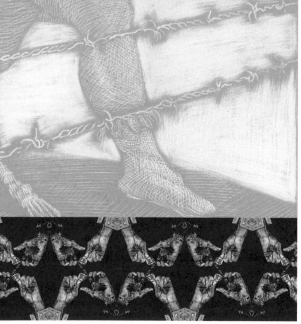

They take up one lane of the state highway as they walk with gallon water jugs in their hands. The blue sky glows overhead, the air fresh with early morning promise. They have walked twenty miles through grasslands, valleys, and mountains. They are dressed in black, the best color for night work. Each man carried a hundred pounds in a backpack. These loads are now neatly stacked in the mesquite thicket just off the pavement. Men with AK-47s guard this stash. A car will come, a truck will come, the kilos will be loaded and on their way.

The men in black barely move aside as I slow my pickup. They laugh and smile and wave their water jugs. They are heading home. Soon the Border Patrol will cruise down the highway, spot them and take them to the frontier and toss them back into Mexico. It all amounts to a free ride after a hard night of walking.

They can make a thousand dollars a night or more for toting their load.

They walk through borders, they walk through laws. They are on their way to a dream where you live outside the rules and you have a lot of money and you will live

forever, even if you die young. There is a man
called Economic Man and he lives within
the texts of economists where he makes
rational decisions based

on acquiring a lot of
money. And then there
are the men in black who
walk and walk and stack
a load for the money and
God only knows where
it all goes and there is no
tomorrow. But for once,
there truly is a today
and it is good and sweet,
especially in the early morning under blue sky
with the kilos stacked and a paved American
highway snaking through the hills and home
after a hard night's work.

But what they really walk through are the
official ideas about reality and about dreams.

LALO'S SONG

In nineteen ninety-five I resigned from the Federal Highway police

and as I was without a job.

I began working with Jesús Beltrán in drug trafficking.

This person moved approximately three tons of cocaine each month

that entered via a port in the state of Colima.

My function consisted of receiving the containers and I would go to a small town to receive a

fax from Colombia

which specified the quantity of drugs for each person

and which was destined for people in Tijuana, Mexicali, Culiacán, Ciudad Juárez,

and Guadalajara

which is why I needed to talk via telephone with the owners in order to

distribute the drug

and they already knew what kind of vehicle they needed in order to receive it.

Because Jesús Beltrán started to get jealous of my relationship with the Colombians in nineteen

ninety-eight

I stopped working for him.

I came to know Heriberto Santillán who had been in jail.

Heriberto Santillán wanted to work in drug trafficking with Elías Medina.

But this relationship did not happen because El Chaky told him to stop being a fool

and to work for him and for Vicente Carrillo Fuentes

and that is how we began to work together.

Heriberto sent me a messenger and gave me his telephone number.

I even took him to a Customs Inspection Agent who was allowing drugs to go through.

Heriberto was no longer like he used to be.

He no longer dressed as a cowboy but

rather dressed elegantly

and even wore a gold Rolex watch with diamonds.

Due to this relationship I found out about executions to settle drug trafficking accounts.

THE
CANARY
Serinus canarius

The leaves drink the sun, butterflies float over the piss in the alleys, Juárez sleeps like a lazy dog in the heat. That's when the death house opened for business.

I can't think summer without thinking of George Gershwin, the immigrant's child, the Jew, the white man springing off black music, the most American of songwriters. The man who finally found the skeleton key for his "Rhapsody in Blue" while riding a train to Boston and being snapped into the rhythm of the clacking of the rails under the wheels.

I drink a beer in the heat while illegals bake on the desert floor, I eat the pollution of Juárez while the sun staggers in a brown sky. Summertime is always the best of what might be.

No one plans on dying in summer, everything is fresh and green and the girls swing by in clouds of perfume. Summer denies death, just as fall slowly erodes human hope. And winter can barely be endured.

Nothing on the other side feels better than a cold beer on a summer day. The air is dust and the light is white and yet the beads of moisture form on the bottle, and life is very good. The nights come down like velvet and caress the skin.

A president of the nation south of the river once explained that nothing ever happens in his country . . . until it happens. But this man has been erased from history because his government lost favor and so his words are no longer heeded.

The two cities that face each other across the river share a common trait: whenever something goes wrong, they decide that particular moment is exceptional and not typical. Women vanish off the streets and then turn up raped and murdered. Bodies are found in public places with holes in their heads. Huge slums spread as more and more factories are opened. The air gets more polluted, the water dwindles, the rains do not come. The police take money for executions. The newspapers and television and radio maintain almost complete silence about the cartel. The army runs drugs. All this is portrayed as exceptional.

The house of death, also, is seen as exceptional.

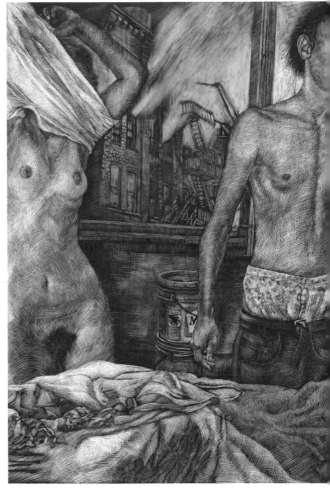

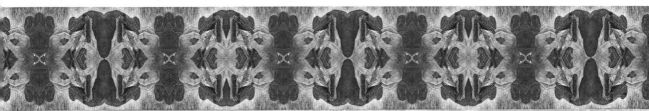

The city thinks of itself as a bustling place with foreign-owned factories where over two hundred thousand people toil. This is a small part of the real work here. The city itself is the factory. It produces the new human beings in quantities far greater than the market can absorb. The giant machines cut the babies from templates of mud, then malnourish them so that their minds and bodies never get too large or free-ranging. By age ten, at the latest, they are fed a diet of paint, glue, drugs, and alcohol. Training in guns and prostitution begins around age fourteen, also tattoos are added to the flesh as adornment. Like the foreign-owned factories, the giant plant of the city works three shifts, a ceaseless production line belching out little humans at the loading dock. There is very little quality control, but even so, some of the production is slaughtered for ill manners or for no reason at all. Schooling is limited since the factory managers believe the product is fully equipped once it leaves the plant. Every year, production quotas are raised and more redundant human beings are fabricated and cast out into the streets.

The noise of all this work is so great that no one ever hears it. They do not hear the screams, the gunshots, the knives sliding into flesh. They do not even notice the work. Instead, everyone says the city is about producing various objects for export—car parts, vacuum cleaners, things like that. Of course, such products are tiny compared to the real production line, the one nobody speaks of, the one slamming out human beings, a factory line of drill presses and lathes and huge stamping devices and intricate wiring and instant delivery. No one on the line gets a bathroom break or any other time off from this conveyor belt of flesh.

So I sit here and seem to be alone as I listen to the clanking in the mill, hear the factory whistle, see the smoke spew out of the stack, watch the new human beings topple off the loading dock and then stagger off with blinking eyes into the city. God only knows who buys this product. All I know is that the production lines never stop, and as I mentioned, each year the managers decide to raise the quotas.

Sometimes I hear this chant in my head, the mere beginning of a song that will someday be on everyone's lips:

No one is illegal.
But we are all criminals.

The first line will be chanted by children, the second by adults. Since we all truly are human and we all truly have human rights and since we all truly help to kill the planet—the skies, the soils, the seas, the giant fish of the vast deep—we all are guilty and when some bestial court is finally called to order, we all will be convicted, amen.

The house of death, a fragment for the indictment—the millions moving north through the dust to escape doom, one more fragment—the drugs flowing north like a river of joy, yes, add that to the indictment. But these are all the little charges dancing around the big charge: planet murder.

Of course, this is a bit severe for us to face and so we invent issues. We war on drugs, we worry about immigration, we wince at the bodies coming out of the ground in the house of death.

CONFISCATED FIREARMS
Ciudad Juárez Morgue

here is an order to things. At the crime scene, yellow tape defines the killing ground. Little plastic kiosks dance on the pavement to mark the location of cartridges and other evidence. Forensic experts make notations on their clipboards. All this information funnels into a system and never again sees the light of day. There is a precise inventory of the caliber of weapons that slaughtered someone, but the guns are never found. There is a precise count of the number of spent brass left at the scene, but the people pulling the triggers move like phantoms through the city. The dead merit an exact description of their clothing, height, and skin color, but their killers remain some vague term like "armed commandos," or, more often, are reduced to nothing but a notation of the color and make of their getaway cars. In the night, police cars race past with light bars flashing. Fire engines charge by in their commitment against flames. Also, there is the order of government offices, public hospitals, parks, and constant pronouncements from the authorities.

Windows have bars. Wealthy enclaves are gated. The rich require bodyguards. Cars are armored. Everything is under lock and key. This is part of the unspoken world, the one outside the yellow tape for the moment, the ground where the next killing stalks. Everything works here, just not the way everyone pretends things work.

Clean clothes dry on barbed wire fences. Sparkling girls emerge at first light from shacks built of pallets stolen from loading docks.

The dead briefly appear in the newspapers, then are not mentioned again. Hardly anyone is ever charged and convictions run close to zero. Things go up and down, just as in the saloons people do alcohol and cocaine.

There is an order to things. Everything works.

The city lives two lives. One looks like order. One feels like decay.

Both are the same place.

Back at the lab, the staff works with giant erasers that obliterate evidence. Bullets are melted down, fingerprints washed away, and the faces on the corpses are ground off until everyone looks like everyone else and then in time, the bodies themselves vanish and no record remains of their passing. The forensics experts wear white smocks and toil in a building the size of an automobile assembly line. Documents burn in giant furnaces, memories vaporize in seething cauldrons stirred with huge paddles. The screams of the murdered are muffled by giant gags of duct tape. Giant hoses constantly wash the floor of the lab and tiny dreams and hopes wash down into grates and are carried off. Huge tanker trucks roll up to the loading dock and all the agony and torture of the city is hauled off to toxic waste dumps. Outside the plant there is perfect silence. The factory has zero emissions.

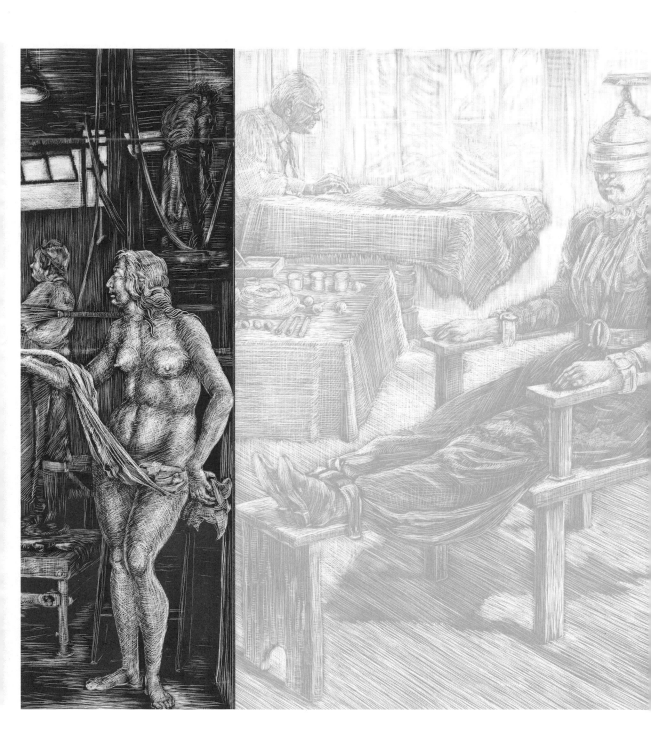

I was first here in this city of the house of death when I was fifteen years old.

I had driven up from the nation's capital far to the south in a converted van such as is normally used for delivering bread. I smoked cheap Oval cigarettes, the common choice of the poor here, and my father sprawled on a cot in the back of the van and drank beer and tequila. The city was much smaller then and greener—the trees long ago vanished as the population mushroomed and the water went away.

The city featured whorehouses for the soldiers stationed just across the river in the nation to the north and it felt like sleep then.

But factories came and people came to work in the factories and then something else happened: people came simply because there was nothing left for them in the nation to the south. And they built shacks along a line between nations and eventually there were at least two million people.

But not when I first saw it as a boy. Then it had trees and the air was scented with raw sewage seeping down the streets.

The chairs in Los Arcos smile with lime and purple and blue. A meal in the fish house runs ten to twenty dollars, champagne can run $160 a bottle. A fully employed person in the city is lucky at this particular moment to make fifty bucks a week. The place is packed with fair-skinned, prosperous Mexicans. Outside, valets park their cars.

The room is tile, voices, the click of a woman's high heels as she is escorted to her table.

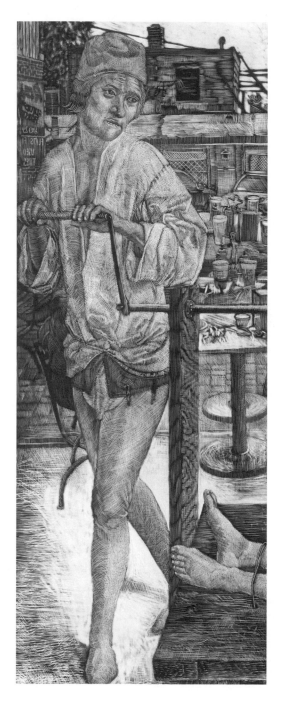

The workers of the death house would meet here to eat and drink and plan their next job, tasks described as *carne asada*s, roughly meaning grilled meat or barbecues. It is a nice place to resolve the humdrum details of kidnapping, torture, murder and burial. The restaurant logo is a happy lobster beating a drum. The tables are crowded with young guys and their girls, the women's trim hips tight in their pants, and all brilliant smiles and midnight eyes.

The voices are light and gay.

This is the skin of the world and this skin covers whatever the world is and will be. This is the face of murder and torture and of love and dreams.

This is the mirror that bounces our lives back at us.

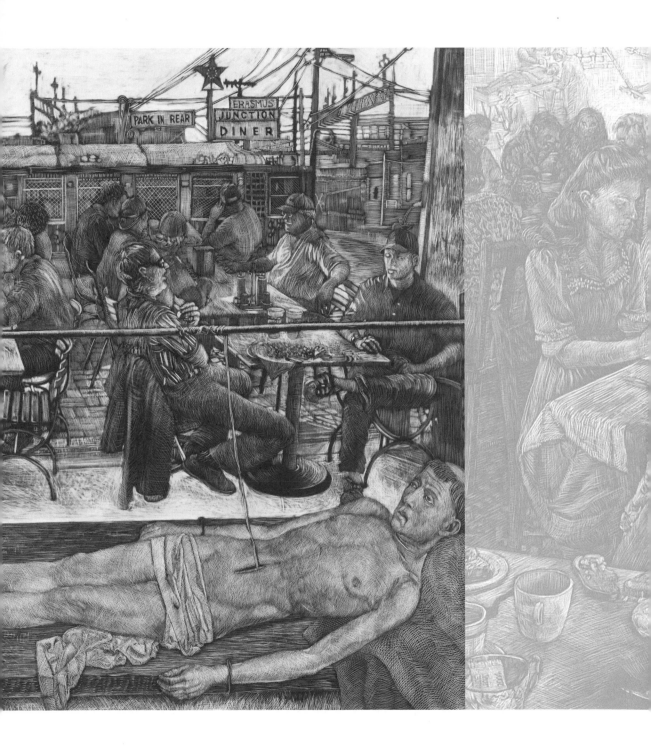

LALO'S SONG

Saúl Aldaña Ramírez drove car

loaded with drugs

to the United States

and Santillán would pick up the cars

and Loya with his people kidnapped and killed Saúl.

The body never appeared.

On that occasion the order came directly from Vicente Carrillo Fuentes

who was angry

because Aldaña was saying that he was buddies with Vicente

although this was simply a pretext

because the objective was to rob him of two thousand pounds of marijuana

distributed in two automobiles.

Santillán told me to set up a meeting with another person

with the last name of Jurado

and later Loya and his people kidnapped him to kill him

but I don't know where they left the body.

Jurado drove a black Cherokee pickup

with license plates from the northern United States.

To accomplish these actions the hired killers used a green Passat

a dark green Suburban

and Loya used a blue Suburban

or the white pickup trucks of the Judicial Police.

Another execution I remember

was about two years ago in Juárez.

by the National Army's theaters

in which they killed two municipal police who were traveling in a Ford Mustang and

they found on them "Cuerno de Chivo," AK-47s.

Miguel Loya participated in that execution

and this caused Loya's image to rise in the organization.

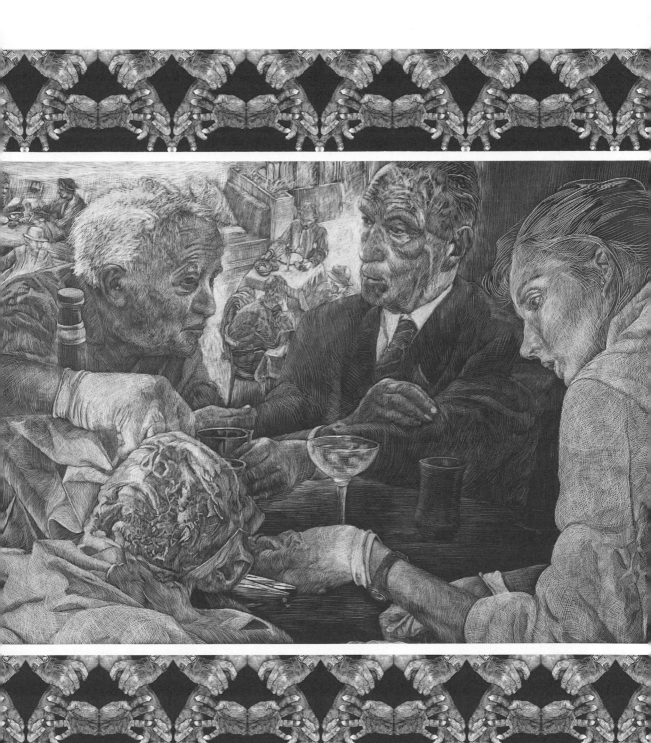

The bright green jacket glows from the side of the trail in the white light of midday. Footprints have pounded the desert soil into a fine dust. I reach down, feel the texture, and then fumble in the pockets and find a new tube of lipstick and a compact of fresh eye shadow. Scent floods my nostrils and I can feel the presence of a woman, her lips roar with color, her eyes beckon. She cares. Before her lie miles of desert, June heat bumping one hundred, darkness and that gallon jug of water tugging in her hand. Maybe her walk means five or ten miles, maybe it means thirty or sixty. Depends on how much she pays. When she pitched her jacket she was maybe a mile north of the line.

Whatever the distance, it once meant she must have her lipstick and eye shadow and then as the branches of the mesquite raked her body, as the night closed in like the lid of a coffin, as the pace never slowed and some fell away and no one cared, as the whole feel of this passage slapped her in the face, then,

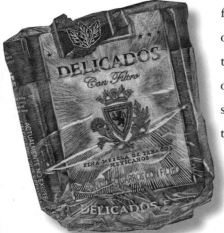

at that moment, she cast the jacket aside and it is a new jacket, one never worn before, one innocent of desert sun with its bright, unfaded green, then at that moment, she became an American, she tasted the new Middle Passage that ground away earlier lives. I look at the compact of eye shadow, little cells with the pebble grain still imprinted on the colors, the brush fresh and only used once it seems. She went forward with her eyes open and beautifully framed.

It is clear from the solitude of the jacket that this was not a pickup point. At such places there is a garbage dump feel of cast-off bottles, garments, and daypacks. No, she seems to have pitched her garment as a personal decision. Of course, when the heat really hits, people shed everything and walk naked for a spell. Then they buckle and writhe on the ground and eat dirt and act as if they are swimming. This is the last phase before all movement ceases.

She is one of hundreds of thousands struggling through this sector of the line. The numbers have become meaningless, as has the passage. It is now a matter murdered by the words *illegal immigration, entrants, humane borders, hold the line*, a series of riffs that have

no consequence on the ground. She has consequence. She will make it or not make it but she is one of half a million to a million who will barrel through this desert gate this year.

I sit in the dirt. The stone footing of an old settler's hut gleams on the hill behind me. The land rolls gentle with grass and mesquite. The deer are down now in the midday heat but they are out there, antelope also. The border is near, but far. Close on the map, but iron fangs on the ground. Leave your car and take a walk and you will soon realize such an act is a mistake. Camp the night, and things could get unpleasant. This is now a no-man's-land where only people with guns have force and anyone else is prey.

You try to grab onto something solid like innocence or ignorance, something that brings peace and soft music and stops the thunder in your head.

You make a list of absolutes, of touchstones, yes, that is it, the kind of list a child could recite like a rosary. You say to yourself:

I know some things for certain.

Nothing will stop people from coming north.

Nothing will ease their pain.

Nothing will stop the violence of the line.

Nothing will stop the drug business.

Nothing will stop my love of this place.

Not even the word nothing.

What's not to love?

Here the lies stop dead in their tracks.

I inhale the perfume rising off the fresh lipstick.

There are too many of us, and so many of us suffer from the weight of numbers on the groaning ground.

I can't decide if I am hearing the cries of a hard birth, or something more like a death rattle.

LALO'S SONG

On another occasion

Santillán mentioned to me

that they killed a person who was one of his workers

and who was called El Gordo, the Fat Man, and whose body appeared

without a head.

On another occasion Santillán mentioned to me

that Rafael Muñoz Talavera

gave an order

to recruit people to hit the people of Carrillo Fuentes.

And Carrillo Fuentes had about seventy people kidnapped from various residences

and in Juárez.

Going back to the executions

on a Saturday in August

Santillán had me go to Restaurante Los Arcos

to introduce me to the lawyer Fernando

where they were having a friendly conversation.

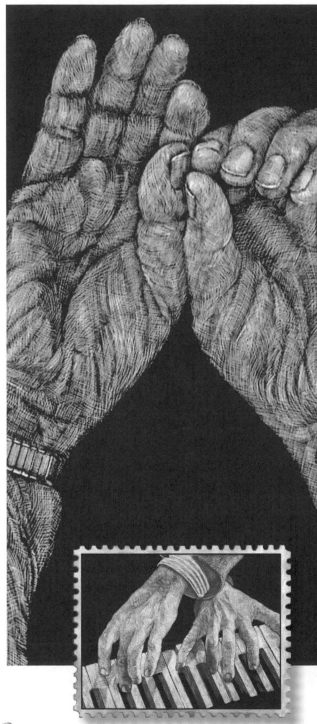

Futurama sells groceries. Nearby is a Peter Piper Pizza. Just to the north is a walled country club where the heads of the Juárez cartel live in calm and play golf. Security vehicles scurry around the perimeter. The clubhouse itself has a beautiful dome. The group would rendezvous in the parking lot of Futurama before proceeding in an orderly fashion to the condo where bodies enriched the soil of the still-barren backyard.

A vendor sells steamed ears of corn, a Church's Chicken fills the air with grease. The street roars in front of the strip commercial plaza. It feels like the nation just to the north across the river, feels like that heart and soul. Nothing bad seems possible on a sunny day under a blue sky on a city street with people carrying bags of groceries and the boys casting yearning eyes at the girls who take in their presence and adamantly refrain from admitting this fact with a glance or a smile. I hear a zim bam boddle-oo song in my head

Li'l David was small, but oh my!

He fought Big Goliath

The air hangs hot and still and empty. I expect to smell something strong but do not. The backyard of the beige two-story townhouse shows neglect, with the dirt churned and not a single living thing. The neighborhood speaks of comfort with a sushi bar a few blocks away in a new Radisson, a nearby Walmart, a beckoning Applebee's. The authorities have come and fetched the bodies. The cadaver dogs have all gone home. People who live here work as middle managers in local factories or other middle-class jobs. The man who owns a grocery store a hundred feet or so down the block and across the street, well, he said he heard nothing. He's anxious for business and recommends his shop with a smile. That is how the calm of a city is preserved: no one ever hears anything. Or sees anything. Or smells anything. Or reports anything.

Coral roses bloom across the street. Neighbors peer out and stare at the house but the street sags under a midday stillness in the warm eighty-degree April air. In the backyard of the house is an abandoned bench car seat, a one-liter bottle of water, and that disturbed soil. A nine-foot wall topped with jagged glass shelters the yard. In the living room of the house old newspapers clutter the dirty cement floor. One corner harbors a press with a metal frame and a big screw jack—ideal for compressing kilos of material into a smaller mass. Nearby are five sacks of cement, apparently for some work in finishing off the back patio that sparkles just beyond the sliding glass doors in the sunlight of this fine spring day.

Between August 5 and January 14 twelve men were tortured, strangled, and buried at the quiet house, and ICE, a component of the new Department of Homeland Security, knew about the killings and did nothing. None of these twelve men were apparently ever missed—the local organization dedicated to tracking humans that vanish here never got a call from any friend or from family. The house is a few miles south of the line.

Officially, it was all a sidebar detail in an investigation of the illegal smuggling of cigarettes. Or a detail in an effort to penetrate the cartel.

Or it was all about nothing.

This latter explanation appeals to me the most because it honestly captures the indifference of two governments to what happened in this plain house on this side street. Years ago I stumbled into this zone of indifference. Today, with the warm sun, the white noise of traffic in the city feels like homecoming. This is not a story, this house explains nothing. This is the world I have come to know and oddly cherish. That is why I have returned to this city. I am looking for my hole in the earth, the one I can crawl into and join the others erased from consciousness.

I feel at peace as I peer into the house of death. I stand in the glare before the humdrum building and a photographer snaps my picture—he will not get out of his car and he keeps the engine running. Three weeks before he was arrested for taking a photograph under similar circumstances. For years, I have heard whispers of people vanishing without a trace. Now I feel I have finally arrived at a ground zero and I can touch the dirt, suck in the hot spring air, listen to the silence, taste the loneliness of this black hole in the body politic. Looking through the open door into the living room it is only twenty or thirty feet to the backyard beckoning beyond the sliding glass doors. To make that journey meant to never come back, to never be missed, to never be reported

missing. It meant obliteration. And now I can touch the portal of this passage.

No one snatched in this city by the drug cartel—or the government employees in the police and army who do their bidding—seems to return. There are no reports from these adventures.

And no one really cares—not in the Mexican government and certainly not in the U.S. government. I have slipped off the official maps and into the geography that is slowly becoming the world. Like some Columbus, I feel a rush as the edge of the planet approaches the prow of my life.

Here is how it works: first some incident, say twelve men buried carefully in the backyard of a condo in a decent neighborhood, catches one's attention. Then one investigates and sees the incident as part of a larger problem. Then one sees the problem as really an issue. Then one sees the issue as really a question that demands a new policy. Then, one feels comfort. Problem/issue/policy defined and question answered. This is the death of the mind that slaughters the intellect of the educated on the line. Sometimes this death comes before anything but little fragments have been examined and the mind dies

wrapped around the notion of, say, the drug war. Or of illegal immigration. Or of trade as embodied in the North American Free Trade Agreement (NAFTA). Cures are suggested: just say no, hire more narcs, an open border, guest worker permits, vigils against violence, poetry readings, plays, magazine stories such as I have written, heralding new horrors to savor.

I've moved into some place beyond that. I am here to announce the obvious, the war. It rages all along the line, it kills thousands, it slaughters beneath notice and it will spill gore on my ground when my bones rest in the brown earth I love. Thirty or forty years from now, the American adventures into the bowels of the Middle East will be forgotten details of a bumbling imperialism. But what took place in this patio, what is taking place all along the line will profoundly alter the future of the United States. The future is here, even though I can't even catch a trace of the rotting bodies with their gaping, toothy mouths.

On the ground at my feet is a Dentyne wrapper that reads: ICE, Arctic Chill, 12 Pieces. I reach down and put it in my pocket as a found poem. I glance up and for the first time notice that the small condo has electric icicles dancing along the top of the second floor, the kind of lights hung to celebrate the coming of the Christ child and the opening of presents.

ICE is the component of Homeland Security that winked at this killing ground. ICE is the cool look at the line that I have come to loathe. And be.

After a while, you find some murders finer than others. You feast on details, technique, little touches of care and expertise. You abhor people killing when drunk or when enraged. This is bad form. You think the house with the bodies in the patio established a higher standard.

You can talk knowingly about these things, prep work on a grave, proper tools for the killing, careful planning to avoid detection. Fine points of the work.

Inside the house lie heaps of clothing, all smeared with soil, garments taken off the dead. Also, there is a shovel leaning against a wall, the tool used to create the graves. An upstairs bedroom has a frieze of soccer balls. Evidently this was planned as the room for a child.

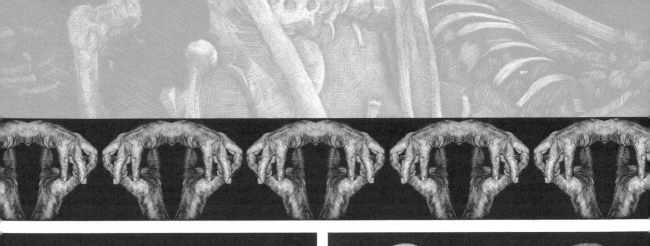

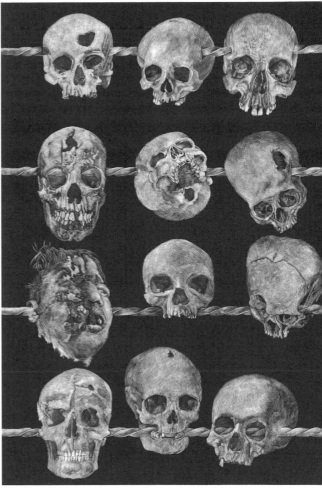

LALO'S SONG

On another matter

Santillán called me sometime later to tell me that in September

César Rubio was already dead

because people from the cartel had followed him

and shot him when he was leaving his house in a Mustang

with his daughter.

He was killed in a Mustang

but I don't remember the street.

Another that I remember, in September

Santillán called to ask me to bury in the little Parsioneros house

a guy who had apparently died of a heart attack

or of a stroke

at the moment he was kidnapped.

I told Alex to send *los topos*, the moles, to bury this person without my having seen the body.

I don't know where or why they kidnapped him, nor who he was and I never saw him.

THE
CANARY
Serinus canarius

48

The bright light fades everything, cars become ghosts, buildings gossamer, the air molten and yet seemingly not there, the dryness also alters things and scent vanishes for long periods and the tongue tastes dust, the black plume streaming from the exhaust of a bus is swallowed by the dust, the green odor of sewage beaten down by the wind, and so everything is brilliantly illuminated but still the eye feels half-blind, distrusts movement, roves warily over faces and cannot come to rest anywhere because some turbulence unnamed and unknown beckons and the body moves, slides down the streets and into cafés and then out again into the dust and light—the signs barely legible in the glare, the sheen of a woman's dress all but erased by the dust, and yet all the signs of reassurance are there, people in dresses and trousers and wearing shoes and watches and stores with flickering televisions for sale and music blaring and trademarks and brands to hold one like a baby and rock one with a lullaby of consumption and ease, the smell of food comes and then is taken down by the dust, dogs look carefully and do not attack nor wag their tails, there is something hanging there, ill-defined but not pleasant,

a possibility dark in the blaze of day, move, move on, ignore this sense, but still it does not leave and follows one everywhere, never leaves once the bridge is crossed and the other nation envelops one with new words and sounds and at the same time caresses dreams with offers of familiar products.

In a nice Mexican bar, the air now cool, the glare gone briefly, a glass in hand, calm, yes calm, music from speakers, yes, look, up there in the corner, music coming from fine and very small speakers made by intelligent men and women in factories with strict quality control, the bass so full, the highs pinging also, a soothing music, and the eyes of everyone in the place seem peaceful, the bartender a smile, the girls in their summer clothes, good wood on the back bar, the mirror clean and polished, the glasses also shine, it is safe but then, the thought comes that only at such moments can you be taken, that it is not the midnight street, the dark alley, the clot of *cholos* leaning against a wall on the corner, the police with their cash-register eyes, the new pickups, huge and with darkened glass, no, it is not these signals of menace that one must be on guard for, it is this moment in the bar, this calm, the music, the bead of moisture slowly trickling down the glass, that is when they will come, you will disappear, yes, you will leave with them, be forced into a car and leave behind you only very vague memories which before the next drink is swallowed will have vanished, it is always when you relax and feel safe in this place that you are no longer safe, that the pain and terror come and to be honest, the thing you have been dodging but waiting for, the credit flashing on the screen that says The End. That is what everyone on every street here knows and waits for and never mentions, no, does not mention once, knock on wood, but still waits for and senses and the air is brilliant, my God the eyes ache from the light and the dust is everywhere and the light is so strong it drowns out all sound and you glide down the *calles* in a gauze of silence as the city roars around you and yet makes hardly a murmur, you glide, I insist on this, you glide.

But you never really relax, no one does. Not here.

Because of the fear. That you cannot say or shake or acknowledge or share or deny or admit.

The dust also. And did I mention the light, that white light from heaven?

If you talk about the killings, you are told you savor the morbid and the dark and that you miss the bright part of life, the bars and dances and smiling children and those roses blooming by the humble home. If you keep silent about the killings, you know that you have become part of them, that you have by your silence endorsed them and the people who commit them.

There is a price for the other reaction.

I once had a friend who dealt with a lot of killings tell me, "The key to survival is exercise. And alcohol."

There is also laughter, that gallows humor that keeps the soul alive in morgues or bloody alleys or lonely rooms with corpses cool to the touch on the carpet.

And everyone agrees the kids are the hardest.

But that is only if you are willing to look.

Should you look away there is also a price, a slow collapse of the senses, a serious shrinkage in this thing we call a soul. The slow but certain stilling of the heart. This latter condition passes unnoticed almost always. It is almost impossible to detect since you will feel like others around you and thus seem normal to yourself and to them.

I remember once reporting on a snatched child and coming back to the newsroom and a woman came up to me and asked about the little girl, "Do you think she is dead?"

And I said, "What in the fuck do you think?"

My voice was very harsh at that moment.

I learned not to let that happen again. Now my voice remains calm, almost soft, and I say, "I don't know. We can only hope."

LALO'S SONG

Another execution that I remember was November 23.

The municipal police of Juárez seized seventy kilograms of marijuana belonging to the commander Miguel Loya.

This seizure caused the death of Paisa and El Chapo

because Santillán ordered me to have these drug mules meet him in the Parsioneros house.

At that time Santillán himself arrived along with Dedos Chuecos, Crooked Fingers,

Erick Can, Loya, and some others.

They were told that the boss was going to arrive.

I told him there that they had to take business with us more seriously.

At that point Loya told them to lift their shirts over their face

so they wouldn't see the boss.

At that point Loya put tape around their head

but they could still breathe and one of them began to moan loudly

so Loya shot him in the head with a pistol with a silencer

but he didn't die immediately.

Upon hearing, the other one began to struggle

and was shot in the head as well.

After they were dead

Alex and I put them under the staircase of the Parsioneros house

and later they were buried.

These were killed because they were careless with their work taking drugs across the border.

Later on Monday December 1 I went to the Parsioneros house

and saw two corpses

THE
CANARY
Serinus canarius

54

and I asked Alex what had happened

and he told me that on Sunday November 30 they were brought by commander Loya.

They were kicking them on the floor until they killed them.

Saddam also hit them with a pistol

and Alex gave him a hammer to hit them because Saddam

wanted to shoot them with a pistol

but that would make too much noise.

The description of the two male victims is as following:

One of them was very thin,

and the other was robust or obese.

The thin one was dressed in cheap clothes

and the other had a sports coat and tennis shoes.

According to what Alex explained to me

these two men

had gone to the AFI offices (the Federal police) in Ciudad Juárez to report the existence

of a warehouse where drugs were stored and which belonged to Saddam

and that Saddam had been warned by elements of the AFI themselves.

I remember that on a Sunday, I believe it was November 30,

Santillán spoke with me

to tell me that he was going to

"grill some meat,"

in other words they were going to kill some people.

informacíon

he oldest body in the backyard was buried precisely five feet and seven inches below the surface. The corpse was in a fetal position, hands tied behind the back, duct tape caressing the mouth. The former head of the cartel once owned a thoroughbred named Silencio, Silence. For a noisy place, the city prides itself on a certain reticence.

When the excavation took place at the condo, the first body was found three feet and three inches below the surface. Land use planning at the site apparently dictated that the dead be stacked one upon the other in the holes. The second day of digging revealed one body. The third day also produced just one. The fourth day brought two bodies into the light, the fifth two bodies, the sixth three bodies, and on the seventh day, just one body.

Of course, the work had been interrupted and the yard was by no means exhausted of space.

I treasured these precise measurements, these units of inches and feet because they made everything orderly and things that are orderly are under control, aren't they?

Once I covered a murder and converted the shots exchanged by the two dead men into foot-pounds of energy, rates of speed, and wrote the whole thing out that way like a kind of aerial ballet. This comforted me but upset others—especially the parts about how many grains of lead tore what size hole at what velocity through human flesh.

LALO'S SONG

Another execution that I remember was on September 11

when I was in Chicago, Illinois.

Santillán called to tell me that they needed the house,

referring to the Parsioneros house,

to "grill some meat"

so I called Alex to take care of this.

Upon returning from Chicago Santillán mentioned to me

that they had killed a person because a mule,

in other words a person who took drugs across the border,

had been arrested on the bridge as he tried to take a load of drugs

and that this person who was arrested

sent his wife to ask him for money to pay for a lawyer

and instead of giving her the money

the dead person killed the wife

and the girl who was three or five years old.

Santillán executed the order in order to earn merit

in that organization

as he has always been willing to do these kinds of jobs.

L et me go deeper into this war. It began before I was born and will roar on after I am dead. It is a collision of cultures. In the nation to the south, a ruling class has run things since before the conquest and the division of wealth has never been fair. Also, the State has always controlled things. Complaints have been answered with force. So the rich get richer, the poor stay poor, and troublesome people tend to vanish.

This was and is the system and it seemed to operate in a relatively stable fashion until human numbers overwhelmed the rate at which the land could feed people. To be sure, there were revolutions but these were met with counterrevolutions and gore and then things calmed down for long spells.

On this side things were more open, there was less regulation and also so much of the ground seemed empty except for Native Americans who were crushed and herded onto reservations. The border itself was far from both capitals, and largely ignored. Few people lived there.

This changed. The borderlands began to fill.

And for various reasons—growing human numbers, failed economic policies, suicidal trade treaties—the nation to the south began to break apart and the poor streamed north and this stream grew and grew into a mighty river of flesh crossing a waterless desert.

But this war I speak of cannot be understood with normal political language of right and left or of capitalism and socialism. It is not postcolonial or precolonial or even colonial. It is life against death. For the poor moving north, it is their life against their death. For the ground and the sky and the rivers, it is slow death as human hungers outstrip the earth's ability to feed them.

There is the technological fix but in the main, this fabled cure has merely accelerated the death of the land by giving human beings the increased ability to grab on and take.

So put a candle in the window and wait for the technological fix.

Drugs are just one more detail in this human migration driven by need.

As things get ever more turbulent, we do need our drugs and so they come along for the ride and color our border with blood and fill the night with screams.

Of course, there is corruption, greed, imperialism, racism, so many words we can fly like pennants in the strong winds whipping now across the deserts of faltering

Pronto será de día
IT WILL SOON BE LIGHT

worlds. We stand out under the moon, drink in hand, and chant these words until our breath fails us and the moon goes down and still everything moves as before and nothing gets better and the footpads of the desperate beat past us into hopes of new lives.

It's a war with no generals and many privates.

There is a new order in the wind and it looks like chaos but it is not. There is a new order in the wind and it sidesteps government, or, if pressed, steps on government. There is a new order in the wind and it cannot be discussed because any discussion might threaten the old order now rolling in the dirt.

 The first killing went down in early August but the condo was by no means simply a slaughterhouse. It had originally been rented by a woman named Erika. In late December, during a pause in the work, she held a fiesta in the backyard for her child's birthday. The clerk at the local market remembers her manner as very normal when she bought the necessary chips and sodas for the party.

The store is new and sparkling clean. It is part of the promise of a modern nation that joins a modern world in modern global trade.

In the afternoon, smoke billows up and strokes the sky. At dusk, the flames can be seen. Then at dawn, the mountain seems at rest, the smoke held down by heavy air, the ten-thousand-foot peaks serene. In 1685, a major fire swept through this range, the Pinaleños. Since then, the trees have thrived, a high-altitude forest of blue spruce and Douglas fir ignoring history on the stone ridge about fifty miles north of the line. Some think Coronado crossed in the valley below or some other nearby valley. Billy the Kid murdered his first man in a saloon at the base of the peaks. These are some of the dribs and drabs of history. The mountain is the long story.

And the long story is unknown to most people these days. A century ago, there were maybe ten million people in the nation to the south, the border an empty zone, the southwest on this side was a place to stash lungers, to pen up asthmatics, and to dig holes in the search for various metals. The line was all but invisible and was crossed freely because no one much cared.

Today, it is an armed camp with millions streaming north, with various organizations

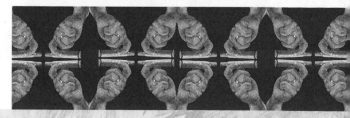

moving flesh and drugs. The fire keeps burning on the mountain and eats centuries of history. The forest itself is a relic from climatic change ten thousand years ago when the world got warm and dry here and the conifers fled to the high ground. Now it is going and no one is certain, under modern climatic conditions, that it will ever return. I drink red wine, watch the smoke billow, see Coronado wander past with greed in his heart, hear the crack of Billy the Kid's pistol, the thud as the man falls. The bottle keeps going down.

There is a red squirrel on the summit, an endangered subspecies. Some years their numbers dip under fifty. In good years, they soar to two or three hundred. This is not a good year. The fire billowing smoke off the mountain is marching through the squirrels' tiny toehold on the summit. Because of a deep drought, scientists have found some squirrels have already abandoned the high ground and its dead trees before the fire, driven down by hunger. Now their empty bellies march before the flame.

Things change, the sun also rises, shit flows downhill and payday is Friday and the fire on the mountain, ah, hear the screams as the flames lick, is a much bigger matter than drugs and illegal immigrants, my God, a world huddled up there like Jews hiding from Nazi storm troopers—a bunch of Anne Franks in the attic of our lives—is dying before my eyes and most likely will never return, a link with woolly mammoths and dire wolves and strange beasts singing as the full moon rises and haunts the land, that universe of dreams and hungers going up like a torch and here on the desert floor, thank the Lord for the wine, red and thick and chock-full of alcohol, down here migrants are creeping north, hundreds of thousands of migrants, that fabled "them," brown, hot and thirsty, the women dragging their lipstick and eye shadow through the new and deadly ground, a multitude coming into my country and nothing is going to stop this, not the Federal agents hiding in the bushes, not the choppers and ground sensors, nothing. At least fifteen million people coming north in the next twenty years or so and Katy bar the door! Because they come and they come and they come, and talk of sealing the border, of humane borders, of worker permits, of different ID documents, all these engaging proposals are like pissing up a rope. They come, the mountain burns, the world shifts, the dire wolf is gone, the moon still rises, Saturday night promises sins, Sunday repentance, and Monday brown people will push the brooms as you pretend they do not exist.

When I was a boy, I thought the world would get better if people only took a good long look at it. Now, no one seems to look. The largest human migration on earth is rumbling past as the forest burns. I can still smell the scent off the lipstick, see the shadow coloring the hopeful eyes.

With wine, I do not hear the babble about humane borders, about worker permits, the screams of the murdered in the drug houses, the panting of the lost ones tasting the heat that has been my life. They will never be cool again, not after meeting my desert. I cannot be cool under any circumstances. I must watch that temper. And keep my hands off guns.

The forest overhead, the new nation marches past. And all I seem to hear are words and then, thank God again for drink, my senses open and the words disappear into the dictionaries where they lead safe and pointless lives.

This fire is the white noise behind the bodies going into the ground in the patio of the house of the dead, behind the people coming north, behind the kilos being backpacked and stuffed into car doors and loaded on semitrucks moving produce, behind everything and over everything is the heat rising in the air and this heat, this warming, it is driving things, making big storms, making long dry periods, destroying villages, turning cattle into bones and hurling people from where they were born toward some place they have never been where they hope to survive.

Yes. This must be kept in mind as the forest burns, the wine goes down in the bottle, and all the little issues buzz around like gnats. Something very big has been let loose and it will rake our hides all the days and nights of our lives.

Of course, the city is more than rented condos used for torture, murder, and burial. In the Los Nogales barrio, the team maintained a normal household, one furnished with good liquor and whores. The neighborhood is pleasant—a former reform governor lives here.

On Avenida Plan de Guadalupe, some bilingual street artist has painted a simple message on a wall: FUCK COPS.

Near here is the house the guys called "Big Brother," and we will get to that house in time.

RIDDLED WITH BULLETS
acribillado

One of the early priests after the conquest of Mexico, Fray Durán, knew the old tongue and listened to the old men and wrote down their tales of what their world had been and what it had meant to them. They had been very rich and feared by other nations. They told the priest of the tribute once brought to their emperor: mantles of various designs and colors, gold, feathers, jewelry, cacao, every eighty days a million Indians trudged in bearing tribute and the list was so complete that even lice and fleas were brought and offered. The tribute collectors told the emperor, "O powerful lord, let not our arrival disturb your powerful heart and peaceful spirit, nor shall we be the cause of some sudden alarm that might provoke an illness for you. You well know that we are your vassals and in your presence we are nothing but rubbish and dirt."

That was half a millennium ago and yet the rich still get tribute and the people who give them tribute feel as dirt and rubbish.

For years and decades, for almost a century, people have looked at this system and sensed change or noticed hopes of change. And yet they all wait for change.

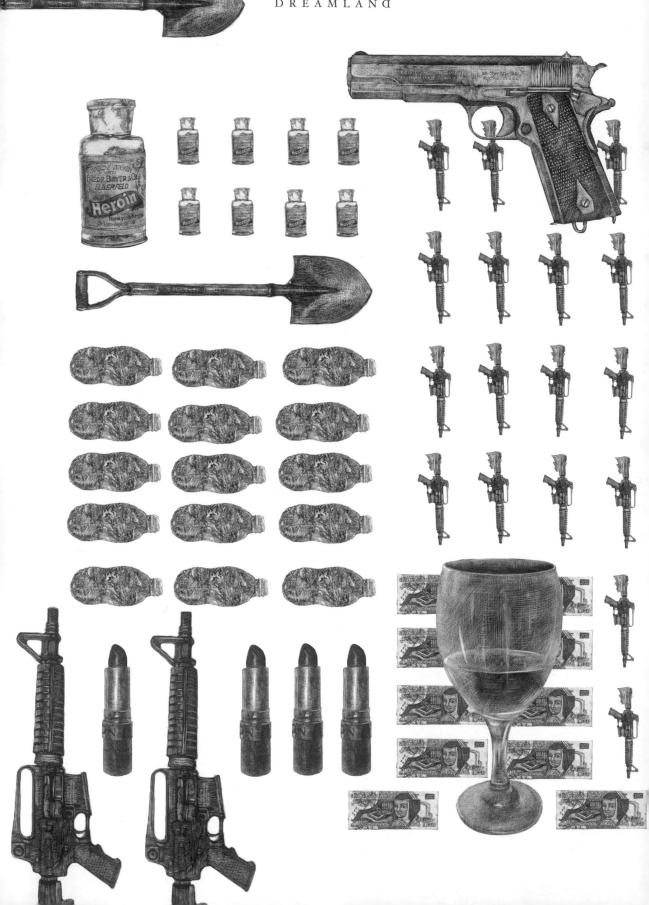

DREAMLAND

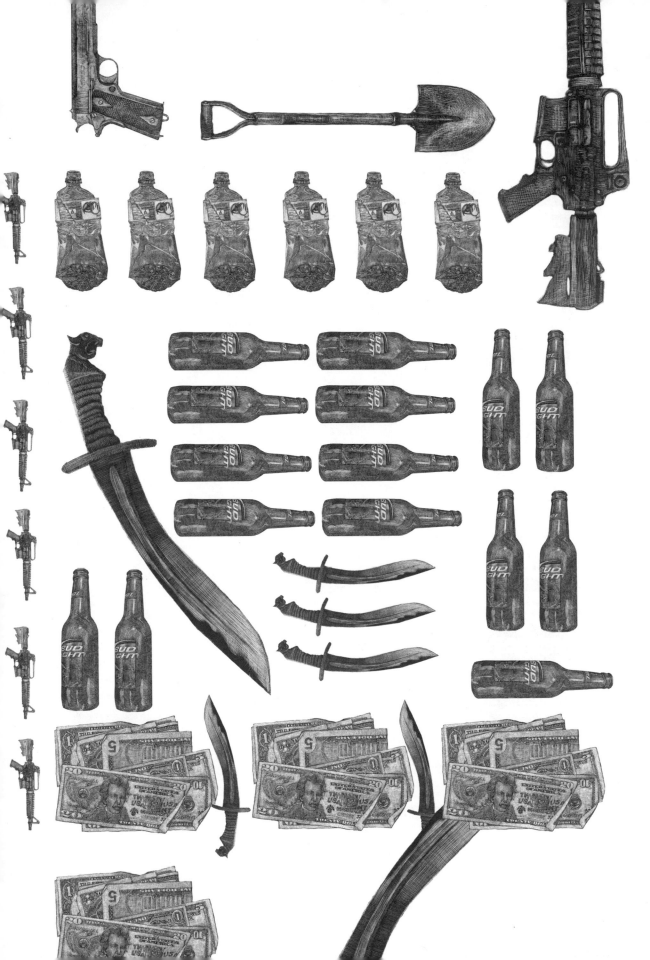

LALO'S SONG

Another execution occurred on January eighth.

Santillán called me around eight in the morning

and told me that he was going to "grill some more meat"

so he asked for the Parsioneros house

and around three p.m. Pérez and Cano arrived

and brought in a person, whose head was covered,

in a white patrol car.

The person they brought had a rope around his neck

and his head was covered

and they threw the body under the staircase.

Then Pérez and Cano told me another one was coming

and about forty-five minutes later Pérez and Cano came back

with another person

who was very large

and was covered in large plastic bags

and who was already dead.

They had to drop this one in the kitchen

because they were struggling to fit him under the staircase.

Later I spoke with Alejandro García

to let him know about the two dead people

and he said that he would dig the hole

because his father was sick

with something relating to his leg

and that it was better for him

because he would make more money.

On that occasion Peréz and Cano

told me that originally there were supposed to be three corpses

but they had taken the two important ones as the other one

got under a pickup truck.
and as they couldn't get him out
they killed him there.
Santillán told me later over the phone that
they had killed these people
because they had been selling cocaine without
the office's permission.
On this occasion I went and bought a tarp to
cover the floor.
I bought eight bags of lime
and went to pick up Alejandro Jr.
leaving him in charge of digging the hole
and burying the bodies.
For the execution on January eighth there
arrived at the house
a policeman who had well-combed hair to kill
the people they had kidnapped.

he first reports from the death house in Juárez were garbled, something about a murder machine run by state police that had by accident come to light and once again proven the deep corruption of law and government in Mexico. Later reports mentioned that an informant for ICE had been part of the killings. The U.S. kindly loaned cadaver dogs to snort out the bodies and it came to notice that such dogs were in short supply because 9/11 had broken their hearts and consumed them wholesale. One such dog at Ground Zero in New York sat down on the rubble after a few hours' work and never worked again. Apparently, the magnitude of the scents overwhelmed his soul.

I got calls and ignored them. I was sick of the border. I sat in a house in West Texas writing a book, cooking dinners, drinking wine, and erasing Juárez from my life. This happens. You get closer and closer and it all feels more and more comfortable and then something happens, you cross some line within yourself and you can no longer tolerate the streets you once ambled, no longer look at the pretty girls without knowing the homes they sleep in. And so, you go away and

try to forget. I remember the cold January day, the call from someone connected to the agencies, the demand I come down and do something. And my refusal and how good the refusal felt after I put down the phone.

Over the months, slowly, the press noticed that the killings in the house were the handiwork of the ICE informant and that the agency knew this but did nothing because they were hell-bent on making a cigarette smuggling case against a quadriplegic in Sunland Park, New Mexico. I am not making this up.

I began to bumble my way into thinking this was my opportunity, at last, to write what I had always known: that the U.S. agencies along the line were corrupt, that the war on terror had heightened this corruption, and that Homeland Security was a mutant agency out of control. In short, I could be a good citizen and point out errors and paste on solutions. I spent weeks in this pursuit meeting people in strange rooms in the U.S. and Mexico, swearing to protect facts or identities, savoring documents, feeling in the know.

Then I broke.

I'm on the patio of an ancient bar in Mesilla, New Mexico, maybe forty miles

north of the line and forty miles from that house where the bodies were buried. A gay vigil is going on in the plaza before me complete with luminarias, paper bags with candles burning within. Dusk is falling, the pinot noir in my hand feels warm and soothing. I could drive and in half an hour be at the home of the quadripelgic cigarette smuggler. I could drive a bit more, cross the bridge and in minutes be back at the death house. Or I could revisit where I spent the day, the living room of Señora Magaña, a woman whose brother-in-law, a Mexican state policeman, vanished about ten years ago, and a woman who eventually became a powerhouse in the matter of missing people in Juárez. No one knows how many people are missing but Señora Magaña has toted up 914. As I mentioned, the twelve in the death house are not on her list.

Her living room was pale green walls, cool tile floors, rosewood furniture, and antiseptically clean. Her face was warm and loving, even when she went off the record and entered into matters that made her weep. She could talk of the police and their refusal to help, talk of the people who call her and their sorrow, talk of how the bodies are burned with tires, or sizzled with acid, or thrown in holes with lime or, according to some rumors, hidden in the walls of mansions downtown as they are constructed.

The señora glowed with intelligence and grit and soul and futility.

I think of her as I watch the vigil in the storybook plaza, a kind of keepsake of a fantasy New Mexico where Spaniards roamed and all was kitsch Indian art, mud houses with rich people and espresso bars, the essential Mesilla, an ethnic prop for educated, affluent Anglos.

That is when I realized I was not in an issue or a problem, I was in a war. I'd just come off of months in Dallas floating around the edges of a fine heroin deal and then settled in to write a book about it. After hundreds of billions of dollars in the war on drugs, here is the reality: heroin in Dallas is $75,000 a kilo, 94 percent pure. So cheap that high school kids can skip the needle and just snort the stuff. Actually, a better deal might be possible since the international heroin broker fronting the load was only paying $58,000 a kilo for the product. Given the quality, a buyer could step on each kilo ten or twenty times. And the supply was functionally endless and waiting in stash houses for delivery. The dead in the patio in Juárez were simply by-products of this war, just as the hundreds of Mexicans who die crossing in my personal patch of desert are simply by-products. As is the Border Patrol itself, a booming agency that keeps adding personnel and keeps facing the fact that every year more Mexicans successfully enter the U.S. illegally.

God, I wish I had drugs that evening in Mesilla. I could have sailed free with a joint.

The machinery clanked in my mind. NAFTA had destroyed the future of peasant agriculture in Mexico and hurled millions toward the fence. NAFTA had spawned a legion of U.S. factories in Mexico and now they were going to China because Mexicans at ten bucks a day wanted too much pay. Nothing on the horizon would alter these facts. Millions were being starved out of their lives in Mexico and coming north. Drugs were simply one more thing accelerated by NAFTA: increased trade meant that searching vehicles for drugs became a mathematical farce. Every year the narc budget increased in the U.S., every year drugs became cheaper in the U.S., every year more people went to prison for drugs in the U.S.

I sip my drink.

The only flaw in my notion is this: the Mexican war is simply part of a global breakdown, the shredding of traditional cultures by the machinery of trade, by overpopulation, by the destruction of natural resources by teeming human numbers. It does not matter if it is a man slipping through the wire with a baby in my desert, or a teenager leaving a village in Eastern Europe for the whorehouses of the West. It is all part of that big picture that wonks tend to in the temples of think tanks. But this one facet, the Mexican war, was happening on my watch, on my ground.

Señora Magaña moves her hands as if in prayer when speaking and her words flow around her clasped hands. On the wall, a gold bas-relief of the Last Supper watches. She explains that whenever she visits the police to report yet another missing person she returns home to find a death threat on her answering machine.

She is quitting the organization now. She can no longer bear the probes into her family's life by dangerous voices. And then she floods the cool room with words, passionate words, and for fifteen minutes she

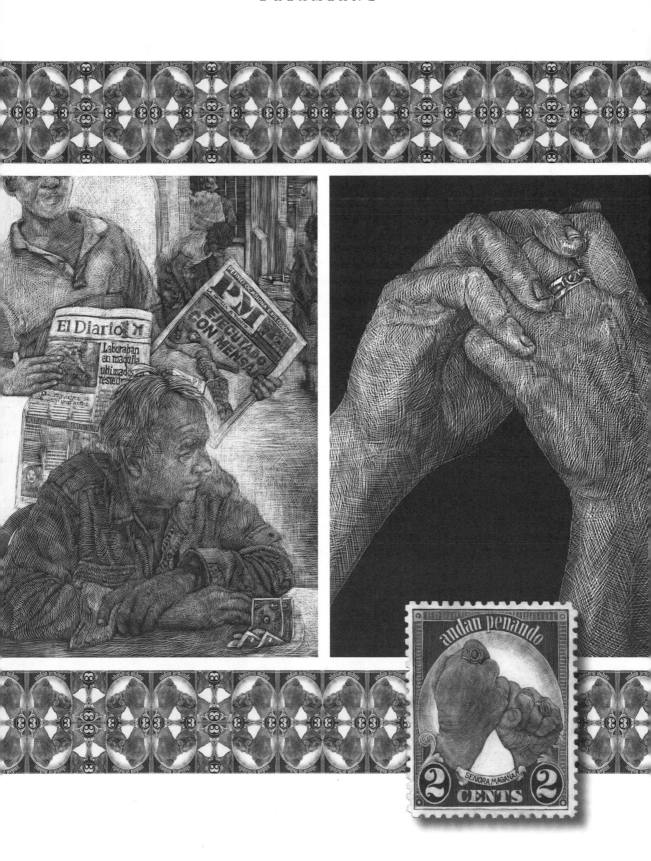

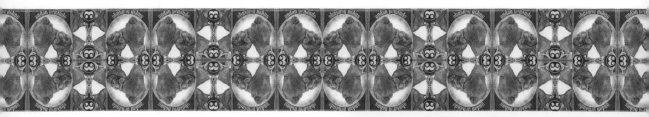

says things she does not want reported and small tears trickle from her eyes.

"The organization," she says softly, "was born in a strange way. A man put an ad in the newspaper that said 'Relatives of the Disappeared People Are Requested to Attend a Meeting'"—and here her praying hands suddenly become clenched fists and then relax into palms once again held together—"and I went and it was like finding the light. Fifty people showed up, and it was August of 1997."

That was one of two pillars that kept her going for seven hard years. The other pillar she explains by pointing with one finger to the ceiling. Then she frowns and suddenly chops downward with her hands. God can seem like a void at times in Juárez.

LALO'S SONG

Regarding the house that I've mentioned as "Big Brother,"
it was used as a guesthouse for the bosses
when they came to visit Juárez.
This house was used for board meetings
or to devise work plans regarding drug trafficking
and the execution of people.
This house was also visited by commander Loya
and they called it "Big Brother"
because those who went in couldn't leave.
They even locked the hit men in this house.

In the Florentine Codex, a record of the Indians' ways that Cortés crushed with his new empire, it is noted that men who die in war go to the house of the sun and then they become birds or butterflies and dance from flower to flower sucking honey. In the old tongue, flower is *xochitl,* death is *miquiztli.*

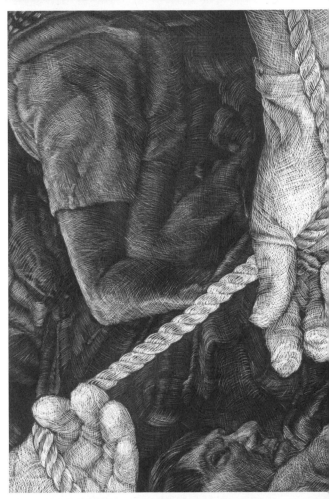

Simple materials can be difficult to find in developing economies. On the day of the first known *carne asada* at the condo, the workers suddenly realized they lacked three essentials of the trade: lime, rope, and duct tape. So they roared around Juárez seeking out these essential goods. The hardware store that served them sells lime at $3.50 for a fifty-pound sack. The place has a comforting feel, the aisles piled high with sledgehammers, paint, cement, air coolers, wood stoves, flues, nails, screws. Here men come for the things necessary for home improvement.

It is essential to be deaf and senseless, or else the things in the air will take us down.

The smell of grease, of eggs frying on a grill, of exhaust hanging just above the pavement, of hammers pounding, of engines firing, of cheap radios blaring, of voices purring and shouting and whispering and chattering, of a city belching and farting and moaning and doing all this while deaf and senseless.

You will never be alone, not here, not even when dead, since we must use space and pile the bodies one atop another to make our ground more efficient.

Cymbal, symbol, the thing itself, ah, that's what is needed, become deaf to all the talk of trade and culture and land of *mañana* and simply see the thing itself and then the hearing comes, that is the gift of the deafness and then, yes, finally the dust settles and you realize you are not in a developing country or a Third World or the past or the future, you are in poverty and it has always been here and nothing has changed it or fixed it or softened it, nothing, not the meetings, the words, the slogans, the treaties, the wars, the revolutions, nothing, and it is not a symbol and it is not a metaphor and it is not colorless or colorful. It is.

The poverty grows, the violence grows, the dust blows and nothing can paper over this fact, not even words like poverty and violence. It floats out there, ignored, a smudge in the dust, yet it is there all the same.

The ideas make us blind, the numbers make us numb, the smells make us retch, and the words make us lie. Imagine a fast-growing city with many factories and almost no unemployment and inside this city people live in poverty and the faster it grows and the more factories that are built the more poor people that appear and the authorities say this is temporary and merely a phase and yet this phase does not end but rolls out like black ribbon and everyone goes down this dark path, carrying those plastic bags of groceries and stumbling through the dust and nothing seems to end but individual lives and these lives are lost, all but erased amid

the births and nothing changes except names and faces and the city keeps growing and the authorities keep repeating "it is temporary" and yet it does not end and now hardly anyone can remember the beginning or imagine a different kind of life.

There is a man running around the city gathering rope, duct tape, and lime and he is of no importance, he is not part of the real present or the real future, he is marginal: this is what we are told. Watch him gather his tools, out there in the smudge we pretend is blue sky.

he glasses are darkly tinted, the hair gray and thinning, the beard full, the voice strong. He sits behind his desk in a windowless room with caricatures of himself on the wall. Jaime Hervella is the man who once stood up. He called a meeting in Juárez one August about the disappeared, and within two years he headed an organization with 196 names of vanished souls. He barks out these facts with a commander's assurance. He is the man. He is in charge. And he is legally blind.

After two years, Hervella stopped taking names. He does not explain this fact. He says not a single case has ever been solved. He says he is now getting excellent help from the Mexican authorities. He hosts the organization in El Paso for safety, in this windowless room of his business.

I listen to the old man talk and talk. I think he tasted the flame and then retreated. I think he tried and I never tried. I think he is afraid. I think only a fool would not be afraid. And I let his deep and comforting voice roll over me. Outside his door a reporter from a Juárez newspaper works at a computer and I can feel the reporter's ears grow to a huge size. Hervella says with a shrug that people

call him about where bodies can be found but they are vague and always refuse to give their names.

I listen to him and I think that he is a man who did far more than I have ever done and then he came to a moment when he decided he could do no more.

Of course, as others tell me, this notion of a war is too strong and must not be spoken of. I understand. I get carried away.

I meet a woman who poked around the disappeared, tried to make note of the missing. She is told by the authorities to abandon this unseemly interest. She nods and persists.

Then her fourteen-year-old daughter is taken and raped.

She weeps as she explains this new reality.

LALO'S SONG

Q. You—you indicated that in Ciudad Juárez that the police were the ones who would do the kidnapping and killing.

A. Yes.

Q. Who were they doing this kidnapping and killing for?

A. Yeah. For the cartel of Juárez, for the chief of the—the bosses of the Juárez cartel.

Q. So the bosses didn't have to actually go out and do the torturing and killing themselves?

A. Yes. Actually, to avoid problems, the police they—they do it. Yeah, because they do know how to avoid, you know, the actual investigations that would come forward.

The rooms at the Radisson go for ninety to one hundred dollars a night and mainly bunk businessmen who have come to Juárez to feast off of the North American Free Trade Agreement. Now the local factories are cutting back as business flees the city for China. On the top floors in the rooms facing east, a fine view of the condo is possible, one that peers right down into the backyard and all that disturbed soil. The lobby warms with soft music and a sushi bar. A café sits under the four-story atrium. Two clocks give local time and Central time. Just to the south is a water park with carnival rides.

On the strip where the hotel looms, the road is lined with Domino's, Peter Piper, McDonald's, Applebee's, Carl's Jr., and Burger King. Every signal meeting the eye says safety. In the midst of this commercial barrage is a club called Hooligan's. One fall a few years back, five men sat at a table there. One danced with a pretty woman. Apparently her boyfriend took offense. The five men left the club but were detained by Mexican police who beat four of them to death. The boyfriend was rumored to have deep ties to the Juárez cartel but this has never been explored and the dead have been

largely forgotten. The boyfriend did marry the pretty woman shortly after the incident, so some good came of the evening.

The nine-year-old boy drives the new Ford Expedition round and round the triangular island of the taco stand. A half block away the elementary school teaches seventy students, some of whom, like the boy, drive new SUVs to class. This is a fragment of the unspoken Mexico, a village called Sásabe, Sonora. I'm with a friend from Juárez but this does not help. No one wants us here. He is a photographer and his camera case slaps residents in the eye as if it were a mark of Satan.

I eat *tacos de cabeza,* head meat scraped off the skull. Dust rises from the dirt street as the boy roars about in his fine machine.

The town, we are told, has twelve major *coyotes,* smugglers of people, and they report to a kingpin. A gaggle of guides works under the *coyotes* and leads the packs of fifteen to twenty people out into the desert for their crossings. The heat is rising as the desert summer comes on. And the heat is rising in the town—my friend spends hours being denied a rented room. No one wants him here, much less me. Traditionally, the village made bricks and had thirty brickyards. Now, maybe three are running. For a spell from the mid-eighties until the late nineties, drugs were a lucrative product. They still move through here but have been overwhelmed in the marketplace by flesh.

There are humdrum glimpses of the life of the immigrants, *pollos* or chickens in the language of the border. Telephone kiosks dot the village but the phones fail after about a minute and the caller must then trek to the main phone office where the rate is five times as high. Rumor says that the owner of that office cuts off lines as soon as a kiosk is used. When my friend tries to make a call from a kiosk, he finds that at least in his case the rumors appear to be true. Nothing is said publicly here and yet nothing is secret. The local grocery is called El Coyote. Packs of humans, twenty or thirty in a bunch, scoot past with daypacks and jugs of water in their hands. They literally scurry to their rendezvous with a guide. Sometimes the coyote supplies American clothing and they change en masse under a tree on the northern edge of the village.

The man running the telephone office seems a cheerful man, writes dispatches for a regional newspaper and knows nothing much of people smuggling and seems very nervous even mentioning the business. Outside his office immigrants sit in the shade. They are dressed in black despite the desert heat: the work is at night.

The immigrants are short and dark, Indians from the south. They are all ages.

A Federal wildlife official a few months before had taken the day off and gone down south of this village where the immigrants get off Mexican buses and queue to take car vans down a fifty-mile dirt track on the final leg of the journey to the border. In one hour, he counted fifty-eight vans, each hauling twenty people at a minimum.

He shook his head at realizing the numbers coming north must be very large and that he would never really get a handle on those numbers. His wildlife refuge faces the village and he has come upon parties of illegals numbering three hundred.

LALO'S SONG

Mark Smith, television producer: They want you deported, and the likelihood is what? And if you go to Mexico, the likelihood is what?

Lalo: Do you got any—do you really think in Mexico you're going to survive after you infiltrate the cartel and the Mexican government and show the proofs that the Mexican government is like this with the cartel? [2]

Smith: How long do you think you'd live if you went to Mexico?

Lalo: I really don't know. Maybe they want to cover things. They're going to put me in jail. Yeah? And in jail, maybe they're going to say I commit suicide, or maybe they're just going to let me—or maybe I don't even get to jail.

The heat thuds against my head at about 115 degrees. To the west, there is not a residence for one hundred miles, little water, and visitation is strictly regulated by federal permits lest this wilderness and gunnery range be disturbed by human carelessness. This is a patch of southwestern Arizona that is unvisited by tourists and uncrossed by normal roads.

They die here each summer, people coming north into an inferno. The Border Patrol hunts them and saves them on occasion. Still, they come, and warnings and death hardly register against the great need of the men, women, and children coming north.

More than twenty years ago, on one fine June day, I crossed with them and after forty-five miles walked out and was grateful to still be alive. Nothing has changed since then except the numbers trudging north. I stare out into the heat and I think that I have learned nothing since that night of fire. Now some people put out water stations for them and this cannot hurt. There are publicity campaigns to warn immigrants away from this route.

But as I stand here and weave in the heat I know they are out there and I know what they are feeling, at least a part of it. I know the pain part, I don't know the fugitive part. My passage was for a newspaper story, one that resulted in nothing but my own blooding.

I want it made a national park. I want it cherished. But also I want it to cease to exist as a killing ground, as a hell where the weak falter and struggle and die. I have blundered into it on foot more times than I can remember and I'd be happy to die and spend my slice of eternity under its honest sun.

A friend is buried out there, illegally of course, but then almost all the dead out there in the thousands of empty miles are illegal.

Here the Mexican war is as soft and polite as the last faint shudder of a death rattle.

They come north into this inferno to smuggle drugs because U.S. citizens wish to consume drugs. The come north into this inferno seeking jobs because U.S. citizens need people for jobs that pay low wages. That is the cause, in good part, of this Mexican war. They come north because we beckon but we do not like to admit this fact nor do we like the people who come north.

No one I know will admit the facts of this war. It is seen as a problem, and various solutions are proposed—new regulations,

new permits, new controls. And it does not matter if the issue at hand is a truckload of dope, a death house winked at in Juárez by a U.S. agency, or a flood of poor people bumbling toward some promised land, still the response is the same, that the problem has a rational solution.

I think otherwise. I think I am looking at the solution and it is agony under the sun, a body in a fetal position precisely five feet and seven inches below the surface of a backyard in a nice neighborhood, agents making busts and herding brown people into vans. I know if I walk down from the knoll where I stand in the heat I will find footprints in the wash, all heading one direction, north. I've walked my miles in their shoes and I have nothing more to say of the matter. The answers are as plain as this brutal afternoon in the sun.

The U.S. government brings values to the line and these values melt in this sun. I love the sun, but my God, it can kill you.

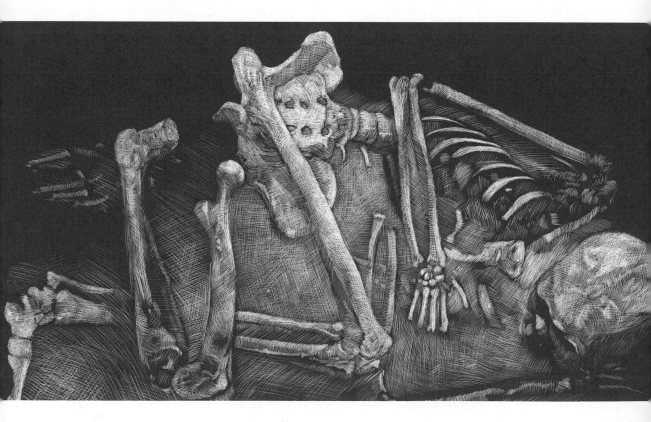

LALO'S SONG

Lalo: Now, it's well known—and this group too, yeah—that in the—in the—in the mafia, if you don't do exactly what you've been told, you get killed, yeah?

Like some of these guys, yeah? So you cannot go infiltrate the mafia, say, yeah, yeah, yeah, yeah, I'm so special; I'm going to do what I want to do, and you're going to play by my own rules, because I'm in the—part of the government, and—you cannot do that, because you'll get killed, yeah.

If they order to you, do this, you do it, and you'd better do it; and if you don't do it, you get killed.

. . . This first time, when I saw the killing, yeah, it—what can I do? Call the police? The police was already there. The police kill him, yeah? So who you going to call? Am I going to pull my gun and shoot the policeman? So then I'm going to be a police killer, and they're going to kill me anyway, because they got AK-47 with them, yeah?

. . . And then I want to show, yeah, what is really happening in my country, because maybe if I just—if I just tell them, if I just say by my words, anything, the Mexican police are the killers and the mobsters, nobody going to believe me, right?

. . . And we are just looking at one cell of one cartel, yeah? In Mexico, there's more cartels with more cells. There's thousands of people who are doing this, yeah?

here is another problem. To speak is to sound racist or to sound anti-Mexican or to sound anti-American or to sound inhumane or to sound foolish. One must face facts. The world is changing and change is pain and there is the matter of bootstraps and the stories of our own immigrant ancestors and it will all work out and something will turn up.

I am told these things.

But I fail in these lessons.

o one seems to have kept count. There are men, women, and children, fifty to one hundred at a time. When the bodies were disinterred from the death house and taken to the morgue the people simply showed up and formed long lines. They came from various parts of Mexico and distant U.S. cities. They stood in line for at least six days. Photographers found the people in the lines did not want to have their pictures taken. They had come to claim their dead but they did not wish their names or stories to be known. They would hug each other and cry.

There were only twelve bodies to identify but so many people showed up looking for their missing ones. Day after day. Families would also come to the death house and sometimes the Federal police would let them in for a quick look. Afterwards, the families always fled, walking very fast. Neighbors would watch, children kept playing, and overhead a police helicopter kept circling and videotaping the reporters who were kept corralled out on the street. Cops guarding the house took still photographs of the press.

And then it was over and no one had to think any longer about how many people may have gone missing in Juárez. Thirteen Chihuahua state policemen were arrested once the digging began at the house and four more were being sought. Ten city cops failed to show up for work once the digging began. The Chihuahua state police department was the agency responsible for investigating kidnappings and murders in the city.

Señora Magaña said, "We cannot claim a triumph. The abducted and disappeared never show up alive."

LALO'S SONG

Mark Smith: What was the Parsioneros house like? Didn't it smell like crazy?

Lalo: No.

Smith: Can you describe it? It didn't? With bodies being drug underneath the staircase, blood—

Lalo: No, you prepare everything.

Smith: It isn't—when you enter in there, you wouldn't suspect it was a—a torture house if you walked in there?

Lalo: If you—in the first place, you don't go there if you weren't part of the mafia, yeah? You have to do something with the mafia, yeah?

And this is the scary thing and this is what the people don't—don't understand. You inside of that house, yeah, like all of us, all friends, all—all accomplices—all the same mobsters, yeah, one or two or four or—I don't know—are not coming out, yeah.

You are not going there with a—this is the scary thing. And no one—and this is very—I saw it in the faces of all—even the cops—everyone has got fear when go inside that house, because nobody knows who's the one who's going to walk out.

Smith: You never knew?

Lalo: You never know. All of us were buddies. And then inside, I was, hey, what's going on with this? Oh, this, this, this. Sometimes okay; everybody walks out, no problem. But sometimes when this man was there, you didn't know.

And I have to say this, I got a lot of guilty for be—for be killed there. Why? Because I was working for the U.S. government. So I was a lot of basis to be scared every time we go inside that house. I don't know if they found—if they discovered what I was doing, yeah?

So if the people who doesn't do nothing bad or supposedly nothing bad were scared, imagine me when I was no—I was betraying them, so—

THE
CANARY
Serinus canarius

102

If you wish to do business you will pay a bribe. If you wish to feel safe, you will not call the police. If you prosper, you will move into a gated community. If you prosper even more, you will have a bodyguard and bulletproof vehicle. If you prosper even more, you will, of course, leave the country. The publisher of the local newspaper lives across the river and in another country for reasons of safety. This is accepted as part of the natural order.

You will almost certainly be employed since by official rules anyone working one hour a week is employed according to the authorities. Unless you are very unusual, your employment will never pay you enough to live on and so you will live with others and pool your money and barely squeak by. Or you will enter a business that pays more but has very poor retirement plans. In this business, if you fail, you are killed. And if you perform properly, you will eventually be killed. That is the nature of the business.

If you are a committed criminal of talent, you will almost certainly hold an officer's rank in the Federal police. Should you rise to an executive level in crime, your bodyguards will be police. Your colleagues will often be army generals. This will also never be discussed. Part of the order is maintained by pretending there is a different order called the government. Everyone knows the government is actually a fantasy and the cartels are actually real but public order depends on denying both of these facts.

There is a belief by some that things are breaking down. This is false. There is a belief by others that things are getting better. This is false.

Order depends on things staying the same with the only changes happening in the personnel—which is constantly shifting due to homicide.

There is no chaos permitted. There is only order, and order shackles all efforts at any other kind of life.

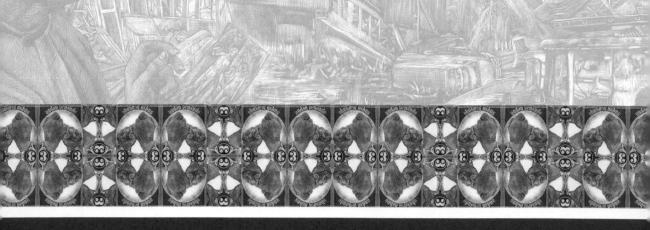

hey shower Cortés with wealth—gold, jewels, feathers, clothing. And young girls who are very beautiful and wear plumage. Their hair hung down, the cheeks painted, and the soldiers relished this generosity by the people. Here the good Father Durán chokes and does not quite give the meaning of the moment when iron met obsidian and obsidian offered up its women.

In that time, when a young girl had her cheeks painted red she was a virgin and about to meet her husband or go with a god. One of the soldiers of Cortés, Bernal Díaz, wrote that when the girls were given, the Spaniards were told this is so they could be brothers and the young fragrant women were to be brides.

But red on the cheeks had power. Whores wore red. Fathers warned daughters never to color their cheeks except for the bridal bed or for the gods. There was a goddess of plants, Xochiquetzal, and her cheeks were also red. But then she was, in addition, the goddess of whores.

So it tangles up together, soldiers, virgins, blood, whores, red, the gods, a bundle of passion that can only be accepted if proper, or damned if free appetite. Blood on the floor of the house in Juárez, red on the cheeks of a woman walking the *calles* and smiling at life itself.

LALO'S SONG

Smith: You kind of—you made sure that they buried them, right? Is that fair—

Lalo: Yeah.

Smith: Did you—I mean what—that was part of your job?

Lalo: Yeah, yeah, because they—they doesn't want—I get a level of confidence—confidence, yeah? So what they—what they used me is like if someone stirs the—or something is—when someone stirs the water, I have to go there and see everything gets clear, yeah?

Smith: Yeah.

Lalo: Is that—does that make sense?

Smith: I understand.

Lalo: So the—the boss doesn't—doesn't going to bother to see if they really—really covered the bodies, did a good job or not, yeah? That was my job, to go and watch if they do okay, and just take care the people are not doing stupid things, right, like playing with the bodies or something to make them discovered, little things like that.

I never take a—a shovel—is that what you say?—or make a dig or move a body. No, no, no, no. That was not my job. I got—I got some level.

THE CANARY

Serinus canarius

No one comes back. They disappear, often reported to be in the company of police. The system is flawless. No one comes back. It is seen as a police problem, or a drug problem, or a border problem. But always it is seen as a problem. This is a deliberate misunderstanding. It is not a problem. It is. Hardly anyone knows exactly what is happening but everyone understands what is happening. A person commits an error, gets picked up, and is never seen again. The nature of the error is of no importance since such errors can never be rectified. The torture, the death, the hole in the ground.

But that summer—it is hot and the world is white with light. Heriberto Santillán Tabares on July 31, a Thursday, bumps into his childhood friend Fernando at Los Arcos restaurant, the fine dining place with bright chairs. Fernando is a lawyer out of Durango and the two men try to catch up on each other's lives but time is not sufficient and so they agree to meet again the next day. The next evening the good times continue and Santillán calls Lalo, the man sprung just a few weeks earlier by the Federal attorney in El Paso when he was snared moving marijuana in southern New Mexico. Lalo of course complies, crosses the bridge from El Paso into Juárez and is met at the Futurama grocery store parking lot by yet another pal who supplies him with a 9mm Beretta with a fifteen-round clip. At Los Arcos they all get down to good drink and food. When the restaurant closes at midnight, no one wants to lose the feel of the fine night and so they head for a bar and the partying goes on into the early hours. Fernando has a thousand pounds of marijuana he wishes to cross and his old friend Santillán knows how to do such things.

Later that Saturday, Lalo returns to Juárez and meets again with Santillán and Fernando. Lalo is told in a private conversation with Santillán that they are going to rip off the half ton of marijuana and a hint of an execution hangs in the air.

The next day, the Sabbath, Lalo meets with Fernando at a Starbucks in an El Paso mall. For about half an hour they talk about moving the marijuana to New York. Others are present and everything looks like a team effort.

The following Monday, Lalo explains the setup to Santillán who remarks that "one would have to be out of the equation," meaning murdered.

Tuesday, August 5, Lalo gets another call

at 9 a.m. to come to Juárez. He complies but once he arrives at the meeting he turns on his cell phone and by that act broadcasts

the events of the day. Santillán explains that they are going to kill Fernando, his childhood friend, and that Lalo is to go to a house with two state policemen to prepare for the

murder. First, he and Santillán hit a pharmacy and buy some hydrogen peroxide and gauze for Fernando's mouth.

Then Lalo and two state policemen go to the house, the cops armed with an AK-47. But the residence lacks bags of lime and duct tape so Lalo goes off on this errand. He returns with supplies about 11:15. He and the cops engage in shoptalk. Lalo points out that gunfire might disturb the neighbors and so they search the condo for some rope, or a club. Also, everyone is thirsty and Lalo decides to make a quick trip to the market for something to drink.

But then Santillán and Fernando arrive with another gunman.

Fernando sits down in the only chair in the living room and begins searching his wallet for the phone numbers needed for the delivery of the load into El Paso. Santillán leaves.

The gunman left behind by Santillán asks Fernando for some coke and Fernando says he has some but first wants to find those phone numbers.

Then the gunman puts a pistol to the side of Fernando's head.

The man pauses in his search of his wallet and screams, "Why? Please don't kill me."

At this point, the two Chihuahua state policemen emerge from hiding.

One shoves some duct tape into Fernando's mouth.

The other wraps Fernando's head with tape, an act that causes Fernando to fight back.

The taping continues in the hope that Fernando will be smothered. The two cops and the gunman force him to the floor and tape his hands in order to calm him. Then Fernando begins to kick, so his legs are taped together.

An extension cord is pulled tight on Fernando's neck, but it breaks. One of the cops asks, "Now what?"

Lalo points to a plastic bag that is then placed over Fernando's head and taped down fast.

Slowly, Fernando's movements

ebb as the group watches. Finally, one cop takes a shovel, gives Fernando a good whack on the back of the neck, and he finally becomes still.

Lalo steps out of the condo to give Santillán an update and finally finds him around the corner at the market. They go back to the condo and look at the body, now moved off to one side of the room and covered with some cardboard. The two cops and gunman are told to take care of the body. The sacks of lime had been carried into the house earlier.

Santillán and Lalo leave and Lalo is complimented on his sound work and told he might even get to meet the head of the cartel. But for the moment, they drive to the safe house in Los Nogales, the one stocked with good drink and fine women. The cops are paid $2000 for their work. And Lalo, after some celebrating, returns to El Paso.

Because he left his cell phone on, the entire day's work had been broadcast. And because of this circumstance, Fernando became the only person who has ever disappeared in Juárez who actually managed in some way, a matter of record this time, to come back.

Finally, on August 25, ICE, the immigration and customs branch of Homeland Security, committed this broadcast in a mutilated form to a memorandum and it went to sleep in the federal files. The memo minimizes Lalo's part in the killing and fudges other facts. Santillán is promoted in the Federal file to being number four in the Juárez cartel rather than being the middle management worker bee that he was. The memo is not shared with other agencies, even though the DEA, the FBI, ICE, the U.S. Attorney's office, and the Mexican Federal police were all cooperating at the time on Operation Sky High, a task force to penetrate and maim the Juárez cartel.

Normally, the memo would have slept forever in the files, like all the other bits of lost history along the U.S./Mexico border. After all, ICE had over two hundred reports on Santillán, Lalo, and their busy cell, none of which ever escaped the silence of their files.

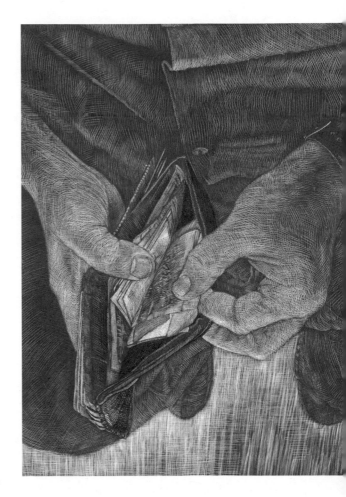

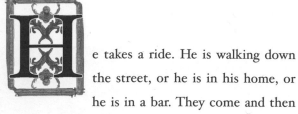e takes a ride. He is walking down the street, or he is in his home, or he is in a bar. They come and then he takes a ride. I've known him for years and sometimes he is around and sometimes he cannot be found. He never explains his absences. For years, he's been moving loads and he has never been busted.

But now he is behind on the money. He owes for a load and so they come and take him. He sits in a chair at a ranch. They are outside, drinking scotch, doing lines of cocaine. His partner is to come with the money. That is the understanding, and while everyone waits, they enjoy that drink, feel the rush of the cocaine. For two days, the time passes this way. They sit outside. In front of him, a guy takes a sharp knife. A hog is strung up in front of him as he sits in his chair. First, the throat is slit. Then the belly is cut open and the guts spill out.

It goes that way, hour after hour.

Later, he says, you know, I thought I could wind up like that hog.

But his partner gets the money together, comes down and pays for the load, and he is set free. No hard feelings.

Soon, the kidnapping, the cocaine and scotch, the hard wooden chair, the hog swinging before his eyes, the spurt of blood as the throat is slashed, all these things are just memories and sometimes simply the props for an entertaining story to tell other people.

That is how it works. Most of the time, you are certain it can never happen to you because you are too smart or you are too careful or you are too lucky. And so you don't worry because these things happen to other people. When it begins to happen to you, when you can feel yourself sliding down into some pit, you think something will bail you out, save you. And when you get out alive, you push the memory away.

Because life is a dream. The money is very good, the deals keep coming, you hardly know how to do anything else. And you have become used to being someone, to being a person in this place of dreams.

So you refuse to wake up.

The wide-awake people seem like living death to your eyes.

All this must be remembered, the love, the dust, the moments of beauty. The city is not simply the house of death, no, no, no, rest assured we have our good moments, and from time to time forget for a spell what we know is going on around us.

I have sat in patios where flowers bloomed and women smiled and the food tasted very good and the wine glowed in the glass. I have seen a friend robbed and he went to the police even though he knew the police worked with the robbers. He went to the police because, against our better instincts, we feel the need at times to believe that there is order and justice in our lives. Of course, the police were of no help, but still, he went to them. We all must do this now and then to stay sane. Just as the woman who kept the list of the disappeared would go to the police with each new name and come home to obscene messages on her answering machine that she knew were made by the very same police. I am completely in favor of this folly. I share the need to stay sane.

So no matter what is said about this place and all the other places like it, places that are growing and pop-ping up to astound us, still the objection can be made and will be made that there are good times in these places and good people and hopes and dreams. And this is true, always true, true in Berlin in the winter of '44, true in Leningrad during the siege, true in every hell humans manage to engineer. And beside the point.

And the point is this: we are creating poverty that exceeds the ability of the State to alter it, we are creating violence that exceeds the violence of the State itself, we are creating lawlessness faster and over more territory than we are creating law. We must ask ourselves this simple question: Is the house of death the problem or the actual solution? Is this the freak show or the future? Are these men monsters or the coming human beings?

Turn on the screen, look at the faces of your rulers, listen to their messages. Say: freaks or monsters or the coming human beings.

LALO'S SONG

Smith: How close did you get to Vicente Carrillo Fuentes? How close were you?

Lalo: No, not—not close. I never seen him. I didn't know him. I never got close to him.

Smith: Is he that insulated? I mean, I thought maybe you were pretty close.

Lalo: No, no. This—it's very—there's—there's a lot of levels and—and he's—he's the boss. He's the cartel, yeah? He's not—he's not dealing with people. He got his—the people he trusts. He's—he saw just the big guys, and I know—I wasn't one of them.

Riding in the night through the ruined ground, power out, homes flattened, people staring blankly into the moonless sky, and Biker Bob says of the city where Lalo and the house of death flourished, "I want to make sure that that cannot come here," and as he speaks men are moving out of villages far to the south, men with brown skin who speak little or no English, they are moving to come to his place and work to rebuild this ruin. And the ruin is from hurricanes and the ruin is from the beating given by modern life. The delta took six thousand years to build, seventy-five years to destroy, and now in maybe ten years it will be too late for anything but doom. The sea is rising, the bayous dying from canals dug willy-nilly, from ill-thought shipping channels, from a change in the weather that melts ice at the poles and whips out monster storms on the deep. Biker Bob is living in a looming charnel house but still he says, "I want to make sure that that cannot come here," and he means every word because Juárez, that place, brings out the dread in men's eyes.

Sitting with a cop just across the river in the nation to the north, and he is worried, very worried because of threats from over there and so he has installed alarm systems, video cameras, rolls of razor wire. He thinks it may help though he knows nothing can stop what is over there. He says, "I don't go there anymore," and he has relatives there and speaks the language and knows the *calles* and cafés but no, he does not go there anymore. And the night comes down, a soft dry wind rolls off the dunes and dusts everything and he keeps talking and he has these monitors in his home so that he can keep an eye on anything moving in the dark toward his life.

And the man is getting on, near sixty, and he has a problem: the cartel over there has put out a contract on him and anyone who wants the money must simply kidnap him, bring him south over the bridge, and then deliver him to people who will skin him alive. There is no question of this offer, the agencies have picked it up in the various wiretaps and intercepts. For a while, he had to live in Asia and even there kept a low profile. His problem flowed from many

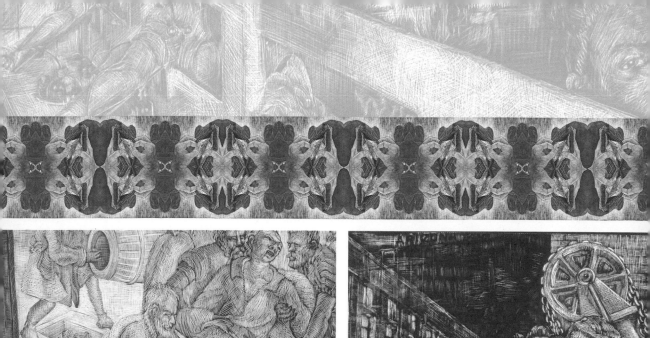

wounds. He was a narc who arrested drug merchants and this earned their ire.

Also, his nephew worked across the river for the cartel and yet this nephew would cross and visit him on his side. On one such trip he stole a photograph of his uncle, the real face of the undercover narc, and he gave it to the cartel who used it as part of the tool kit for vendors who wished to take up the contract for his kidnapping and skinning.

He pauses briefly after explaining his nephew's role and then says, "Don't write that. That's what they think of all of us." And there is no need to ask what they think or even who they might be.

These memories come at odd moments, usually late in the day, or in the dark of night when the machine hurls down the road into the sad hours after midnight. They touch this fear of disorder, of something new coming into being under the sun, some place and people and manner of things that are violent and unruly and beyond the imagination and yet part of a growing dread. Havoc will flood the streets, the wind will come up, the gun will replace the handshake, no one will protect the women, and the children will be roasted on spits by satanic groups who will gather on mesas in the dark of the moon or in forests where even the wolf fears to go.

But instead, a new order grows, one where you are buried in the patio of a condo, one where your childhood friend sets you up, one where duct tape caresses your mouth, a shovel caves in your skull, and lime eats at your body as it returns to earth. A place where young girls are taken off the streets and raped and murdered, where a man sits in a bar over his drink and then vanishes forever in the custody of what looks to be police, where dogs find bones in the desert, where the police are not on the level, the governments lie routinely, the phones go dead, the music grows louder and never stops, and you can go home again but then you may die on the commute.

I think the new order cannot be stopped if the old order continues its retreat. Communities becomes gated, morality becomes police, safety becomes wires and buzzers and not other human beings, the weather becomes something outside and seldom visited, love becomes pornography, speech becomes phone calls, hate becomes anonymous outbursts hurled through computer chips, courage becomes lawyers, and no one ever sleeps on the ground because the beasts wander there at will.

The State persists, just as astrology persists and many things persist, but the State becomes a shadow on the wall that pretends to be in charge. The order now comes from the streets and it is unruly but regular, unfair but as certain as a killing frost and everyone decides this is the way it has always been. The planet slowly heats to a bonfire level and yet everyone says nothing is really new under the sun.

Something, whiff of hellfire or of heaven, something of the future already arrived in the small condo on the side street in the city that causes fear in the heart, the city that cannot be discussed or examined, the city with dust in the air and men and women in the ground.

LALO'S SONG

Smith: Who is it—it says there is no doubt in your mind that other agencies, aside from ICE, knew, knew—

Lalo: Yeah.

Smith: —that there were bodies being buried over there, people dying over at that—that little house—is that what you called it?—you know, for quite some time?

Lalo: Well, people were dying in other cities. You know, they're—that's—it's sad. It is not—it is not a good thing, but that's the—the daily bread over there.

If you saw closely the—the news all the time, they are killing in private or in the street. They don't care. They really don't care.

he killings go on and on, the backyard of the house is sufficient for the cascade of corpses. On January 14, another visitor to the house, while being questioned, offered an address in Juárez. A team left the house and knocked on the door at the address they had been given where they believed large amounts of marijuana were being stashed. The woman inside with her daughters panicked and called her husband who returned home and piled his family into a car. Soon he was stopped by a group of Chihuahuan state policemen and Lalo's helpers. The man held an identification document up to the window. Lalo, when told by phone of these credentials, called his friends at ICE and learned the man in the car with his family was a DEA agent stationed in Juárez. The man being tortured back in the condo had misspoken, perhaps because of stress, had been off a single digit in his address. The house next door to the DEA agent was, it seems, the actual stash house. Also, the agent in the car called his DEA partner on his cell phone and soon he showed up.

This marred the day. The two agents and their families were rescued and taken to El Paso. On January 15, Santillán was arrested and charged with murder. News of the death house erupted into newspapers, and the story of the cigarette smuggling case also appeared and the alleged mastermind, the quadriplegic in southern New Mexico, was arrested. Various Mexican cops were arrested or simply vanished. Commander Loya left and no one knows anything about him. The digging began in the backyard, the lines of hopeful and frightened people began to form at the morgue.

For months, various stories appeared about the case and about the knowledge of ICE and their informant's role but other media ignored these stories. Lalo became a protected witness in the United States. The trials of the cigarette smuggler and Santillán kept getting delayed. The key witness, Lalo, had one liability as a witness: he was a successful serial killer.

Knowledge that at least one American resident alien was among the dead in the backyard led to the filing of a civil suit still pending. The two supervisors of the Lalo cases in ICE were laterally moved. The U.S. Attorney in charge of the whole matter, Johnny Sutton, once a member of the Bush/ Cheney transition team after the election, has

kept silent about the matter. Juanita Fielding, his employee in El Paso and the woman who had Lalo's marijuana arrest quashed in June, remains at her job in the Justice Department. An investigation by DEA and ICE has never been made public. The two DEA agents almost murdered along with their families in Juárez have been reassigned. Eventually, the cigarette smuggler took a five-year sentence as part of a plea bargain, one that saved Lalo the trouble of appearing in court. ICE never permitted DEA to question Lalo alone or to listen to the tapes Lalo had starred in.

At one point, Lalo returned to El Paso, either with the approval of ICE or without it. He was to meet someone from the cartel at a Whataburger. But he sensed danger and sent a friend and the friend was murdered. Two things came out—the suspicion that ICE itself had set Lalo up in order to solve a messy agency problem and, months later, Lalo's statement that his dead friend was, as it happened, an FBI informant.

Twelve to fourteen people died between August 5 and January 14 at the hands or orders of Lalo and Santillán while the cigarette case lumbered toward completion in ICE. On August 11, six days after the initial

carne asada with Fernando, DEA requested a meeting with ICE to discuss that murder. ICE never showed up. DEA wanted Santillán arrested then. ICE declined because of the importance of the cigarette smuggling case. After the death house became public in January 2004, because two DEA agents and their families were almost murdered, the head of ICE in El Paso said he had never known of the August 5 murder of Fernando or the other doings at the death house.

Silence returned to the border.

DIOS CONCEDEME SERENIDAD PARA ACEPTAR LAS COSAS QUE NO PUEDO CAMBIAR

VALOR PARA CAMBIAR LAS QUE SI PUEDO

SABIDURIA PARA DISTINGUIR LA DIFERENCIA

observar en silencio

The man sitting in the motel room leans forward, elbows on knees, and punches down with his hand for emphasis. He is angry at what happened. The open window erupts from time to time with heavy trucks grinding down the road. He ignores the sounds, his eyes gleam, and he keeps talking without pause. He is a man possessed by events. After the two DEA agents were almost slaughtered, the agency's Mexico City station set up an office in El Paso to reconstruct the incident. And discovered their investigation did not jibe with what ICE was saying. Earlier, Attorney General John Ashcroft was reported to be angry over the death house. But when it became a dispute between ICE and DEA, his anger apparently cooled and the wagons circled to protect turf.

Documents ceased to be forthcoming, requests for information went nowhere. For the man sitting in the room, the man who wants his name and rank and agency to remain undisclosed, this was an unbelievable reality. He could live with the system failing, since all systems fail from time to time. But what if he had given his life to a system that was day in and day out a failure? What if he had worked for something corrupt and evil?

His mind could not deny this possibility. But his heart and soul could not accept such a reality.

There are other documents. There are people who might talk. There has to be a way, he insists, to reveal that his government consents to murder and then buries the facts of the murder.

He tells me that what has happened must not be forgotten, tells me this as the tortures and killings and rotting corpses are vanishing from sight within the cobwebs of government files.

A year passes and the death house becomes just another faceless condo in a border city. As I sit there listening, a part of me wants to reach out and strangle the people who desire justice but will not risk their careers over the matter. The people who show me documents but refuse to let me quote them, who have been in the rooms where the death house was argued but will not let such moments be part of the record. I want to strangle them on behalf of all the dead drug dealers, strangle them on behalf of all the missing girls in Juárez, girls whose cases were investigated by the Chihuahuan state police who supplied executioners to the Juárez cartel in the death house, strangle them on behalf of every person living in a shack thanks to a job in an American-owned factory blessed by the free trade agreement, strangle them on behalf of each and every illegal immigrant baking along the line in summer, freezing to death in winter. Strangle them on behalf of the missing, now officially nearing a thousand according to the organizations that track such things in Juárez but whose real number is belied by a simple fact: not one of the twelve men who disappeared into the backyard of the death house was ever reported missing by anyone. Strangle them on behalf of myself and the little count I keep of the thousands of murders along the line because of drugs and drug laws, of the thousands of corpses along the line because of immigration laws.

But I know they are all good men and women and I know that everything I loathe along the line flows from good men and women. It is a system. There is a war on. And this border is a skirmish in this war. The death house is a detail. In fact, the same group had just rented another house three blocks away but the events of January 14 apparently prevented them from fully utilizing this other house. And there are other houses like the death house operating in Juárez at this moment, this is a certainty, and someone in ICE or the DEA or the FBI or the CIA knows of such houses because communications in Juárez are penetrated by a vast array of intercept equipment.

Small improvements could be made in this system. Decent wages paid by American companies in Juárez would lessen the violence and slow or end illegal immigration in that area, but this is impossible because the companies must compete with businesses in Asia. Legalizing drugs would destroy the cartel and end the cash flow into their hands of tens of billions of dollars a year, but this is impossible because American citizens would consume drugs without guilt. Opening government files would prevent future cooperation with killers, but this is impossible because of the need for national security.

And giving secret documents to me is well-nigh impossible, because this would jeopardize careers and pensions and family dreams.

Everything is impossible except the status quo.

I am back on the line where Mexicans trudge through the wildlife refuge seeking the golden shore. I walk the trail where months ago the woman dropped her green jacket with lipstick and eye shadow in the pocket. A doe slips through the mesquite near the burying ground of the old ranch as the afternoon sun runs yellow on the ground. The plastic flowers on the sixteen graves still glow from the Day of the Dead. The line runs a mile or so to the south. A rose-colored knit blouse flaps in the wind on a barbed wire fence along the drag road by the border. Nearby, a small heap of empty water bottles rests in the wash by an abandoned shoulder sack.

The doe's eye gleams with moisture but her moves are caution rather than fear. The brunt of the hunting season is past, the legal guns have fallen silent. I feel like hardening concrete.

A black van lies marooned by the shoulder of the dirt track. The door on the driver's side has holes from six rounds, the other side has three exit holes and two bulges where the bullets lacked the punch to beat their way out. The sixth round could be anywhere, perhaps in soft tissue. The windows are shattered, the tires flat. On the van floor is an empty longneck of Bud Light and a child's red sweatshirt (Fashion Kids, Made in China). Whatever happened here is over and slipping from memory. The wildlife refuge simply lacks the money to haul away all the abandoned vehicles.

The man carrying the baby in the June heat passed by here on his way north. And today hundreds are probably on the march all around me. As are drug smugglers. And vaqueros who cut the border fence in order to graze their stock illegally on the tall grass of the refuge. Earlier I saw one ride by with a child on the saddle before him. The cattle move silently on the slopes facing me.

When I check at the refuge headquarters, no one seems to have any memory of the black van or what happened to it or its driver. It has slipped away, it probably never was the cause of much conversation. Things happen too often to be noted and are erased too swiftly to be remembered.

I am on the hillside, sun in my face, looking south. A short way off, two Border Patrol trucks have blocked the dirt lane. The agents are out running in the desert to the north chasing men, women, and children.

Narcotraficante

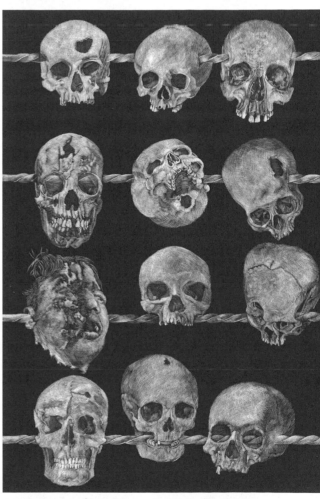

The grass flows golden in the heat and then the rains come, the earth breathes, and the sheet of life goes green and the mat of blades melts borders into a sea of yearning. All along the current line, there are these mesas and valleys where the grass flows and ignores the lines of nations. And the people in the death houses come from here, from these isolated ranchos. And they come from the desert floor below, the *jacales* with a mesquite nearby for shade, those tiny chairs under the tree, the yard around the hut swept clean, and old machines scattered here and there in death grimaces from when that piston flew or that transmission ground to a halt.

The cities also come from these places, as do the killers and people murdered in the death houses and the people killing in the death houses. Just as the homes of slaughter look like every other home on the block, so too does the land surrounding the city look normal and good for the soul. There is no line between the grasslands or the deserts and the grave with a dose of lime, it all flows together and comes from what we are and what the land is and what we have become.

We need a decent X-ray machine, one that can go beyond staring through flesh and seeing bone, one that can unravel more than DNA, one that can capture what we cannot even remember, a ray that sees where we came from and what we have become. A giant Gulliver is strapped to the table, and the Lilliputians lower the lens of the machine and suddenly we see a Clovis spear point tearing into the hide of a woolly mammoth, we see a child smiling at the table as his mother serves him eggs, beans, and a tortilla, and outside the door, that rose blooms and a waft comes off the giant Gulliver and we smell the girls walking by in their summer clothes, the scent of gun oil coming off the barrel, hear the crack of automatic rifle fire, have a huge, four-door pickup with tinted windows streak toward our eyes, notice the kilos piled up neatly, feel the heft of a bag of lime, stop still as we hear the tear of duct tape, the soft moaning of a man suffocating, and a fiesta dances through the body on the table, a narcocorrido roars out of the liver, the prayers of a priest rise up as an undulating voice over a row of corpses in a church, the scrape of the shovel as a new hole is dug in the patio, and birds migrate and come out of Gulliver's mouth, the stars twinkle in his intestines, Venus and Mars are in the same house, the band strikes up and the dance begins, and the grass flows across all lines, the storms roll through, the beasts migrate, buffalo, mammoths, antelope, hummingbirds, killer bees, everything moving and it is all visible, right there on the X-ray plate, frozen in time, but then it shifts and we see more and more and more and we suddenly realize that the house of death is our little house on the prairie and our little house on Elm Street and that it is the entryway and the exit for all our dreams and dreads and limits.

We come from green ground teeming with insects and the earth hums now as the summer rains wash the dust from our eyes and we briefly say life before we return to death.

LALO'S SONG

Lalo: I'm going to be killed. That's not a—that's not a big—a big question. That's what's going to happen.

Smith: You look—you look awful calm for a guy that's talking about this kind of stuff.

Lalo: Well, I got two years thinking on this.

THE
CANARY
Serinus canarius

The planet is being skinned by my kind and this means people leave ancient ground and push out into some void called the future. The Mexican line is simply a detail in this movement and the Mexican war is simply one response, that of government, to a reality that is past denying or changing. Where I sit is the ground from which the lessons have entered my life. I first saw this patch of high-desert grassland and mesquite as a boy and then it was a lonely ground seldom visited and barely noted by mapmakers. Now it is the center of a war room where all kinds of marks on various plans see it as a stream of drugs, blood, and human beings heading north. The little village to the south averages a thousand people a day marching north and remains unknown except to the various forces seeking to control the border. Juárez, to the east, with its noise and slaughter, is simply another glimpse of this same vista, a vista where all can see that the land has failed people due to global trade and destruction of soil and water, a vista where human numbers have exceeded the ability of the earth to sustain them, a vista where criminal activities such as drugs or sex trafficking offer entrepreneurs the chance for success even though they begin with limited capital.

What commentators and politicians call problems are no more than how these facts manifest themselves. There is no drug problem, there is a drug appetite. There is no immigration problem, there is a flight from poverty and a demand for cheap and docile labor. There is no violence problem, there is simply an economic engine running without lubricant and without much hope of lubricant unless you count blood as a possible source, something our ancestors would simply see as a typical unregulated market. And the Mexican war is actual and it is fought by Americans against Mexicans because such a war is preferable to Americans. The only alternative is to recognize the implications of our appetites and policies and no one wishes to do this. On this border it does not matter who is president or which party is in power. On this border the facts remain the same, and the death houses remain open for *carne asada*s.

This is the new geography, one based less on names and places and lines and national boundaries and more on forces and appetites and torrents of people. Some places, parts of

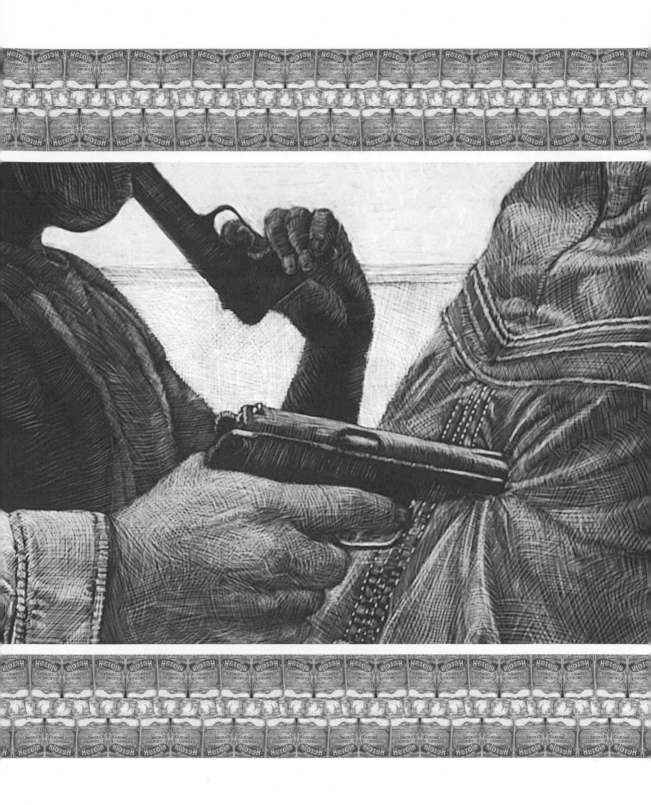

Europe, island states here and there, remain temporarily out of play in this new geography. But the Bermudas of the planet are toppling one by one. The waves wash up now into the most ancient squares by the most solemn cathedrals.

Someday, maybe next week, maybe next month, maybe next year, the black van with the bullet holes will be towed away and no one will have to see it and try to decipher it as a Rosetta Stone of the age. But it will be replaced by other vans with bullet holes. Someday, American military and police units will so dominate this valley that the traffic will move elsewhere. But the traffic will not cease for decades. Just as the death house in Juárez is now an archaeological dig and closed to new customers, other death houses are already opening their doors, hungry for customers.

That is the solution to the problem because there is no problem, there is a market. And nothing will alter this market this year or next year or for decades to come. We have learned to live with the problem

by lying about the problem. There are worse fates, I'm sure, but they must be terrible fates indeed.

The Mexican war continues. Not a single soldier on the line believes in victory, nor does a single general admit defeat.

hey lie naked in the dirt. Their clothing has been stripped from their bodies and buried in a separate hole. Later, this will change—amid a great clamor the dead will be dug up and hauled away from this patio in a nice neighborhood. They will go to that morgue and lie for a spell on cool tables. Hundreds will pass by and hope to catch a glimpse of a loved one, hope to see through the faces of agony to the faces they once kissed and stroked. The clothing will be pitched into one of the rooms in the condo, the shovel caked with dirt will lean against the wall behind them. The jackets of the dead will still boast trendy labels, filthy yes, but still the labels can be discerned and from these messages the dead still speak. They say I mattered, I was in the life, I lived rather than cowered, I had money, I was someone before I became nothing.

But what I think about is not the dirt or the labels or the shovel. I think of the stars. They are lying there, one atop the other to efficiently use the space, their faces duct-taped, hands and feet bound, heads sometimes crushed by wallops from that shovel, but still they lie there and look up and see the stars. Of this, for some reason, I am sure. They see the stars and have the time for once in their . . . in their time on earth to feel the delight and awe that the constellations of the night can bring a soul, that peace that churches try to deliver but cannot, no, this is beyond religion, even if religion came as a reaction to this beyond.

The stars move slowly and quietly overhead, the constellations the men no doubt ignored when they spent their nights in bars and clubs and houses and in trucks with big engines and darkly tinted windows, nights moving around the city, talking on cell phones, maybe doing a line of cocaine to keep alert and to keep the party going. The stars now must surely command their attention, and I hope their eyesight has been improved by murder, that they have the power now to see past the city, to cut through the flow from electric lights, that now they are gifted and can stare into the boiling dots that mean eternity to their species, the stars that guided wise men to Bethlehem, the stars that comfort shepherds and their flocks, that shine on the backs of marauding owls, the stars that twinkle and sometimes seem to blaze, stars that are said to shoot across the sky although this is not

really true—still it is said, the stars that have names and meanings, the hunter Orion, the Big Dipper, so many names because for so long we lived out under the stars and they were our companions and companions must have names, of course, and these same stars tell time for those who keep a close watch, tell time as well as Big Ben, and now the dead have the leisure to learn this fact, to note how the movements of the constellations signal the hour and minute and second, a silent tolling of the bells in the sky, and also, there is the matter of the moon, its phases, its various colors depending upon the time of year, the Comanche moon, the hunter's moon, so much for these men to savor and learn and relish.

The stars rise over Juárez and finally someone notices and feels the grace and peril of the night sky.

That is what I think must have happened in these holes in the patio as the tortured men finally found the space in their hectic lives for the magic of the heavens.

he plaque is brass and newly cast. It is bolted to the death house on Calle Parsioneros and it reads: House of Life. This is a necessary change in terminology. We must shift to this new usage if we are to stop our lying. The plaque will shimmer with dancing light when the electric icicles that line the roof switch on at dusk. The neighbors at first avert their eyes from the new plaque because it questions their necessary fantasy, just as it questions our own. We need to believe that the formerly titled house of death is a spot of unique evil, a place where hell boiled over and the hot lava of sin became visible and forced us all to denounce evil and fix our crooked ways. But, of course, the killings were simply stated facts without apology. The entire neighborhood surrounding the condo is inhabited by middle managers in the maquiladoras, men and women who make their living by supervising other men and women who assemble things for a wage that cannot sustain life. And beyond this neighborhood are the vast *colonias* of shacks where the workers in the factories live and where others come to ground who cannot even earn the hopeless wage offered in the factories.

The house of death, now the house of life, is the truth center for the city, the place where the dead finally can relax and not have lies pounding their rotting ears, the place where no one blames cartels or gangs or anyone but themselves for a city of poverty, crime, violence, and murder.

The brass plaque glows. We must keep it polished as the dead troop in to finally relax in a place where they can shed the fictions of life and bask in the glowing sun of reality. There will be *carne asada*, music in the small hours of the night, light tapping of bony feet as the dances commence. This is the home of the party hardy, the house of life, the house of hope, the house where the future cannot be contained by the frauds of explanation.

Strike up the band.

Shake those bones.

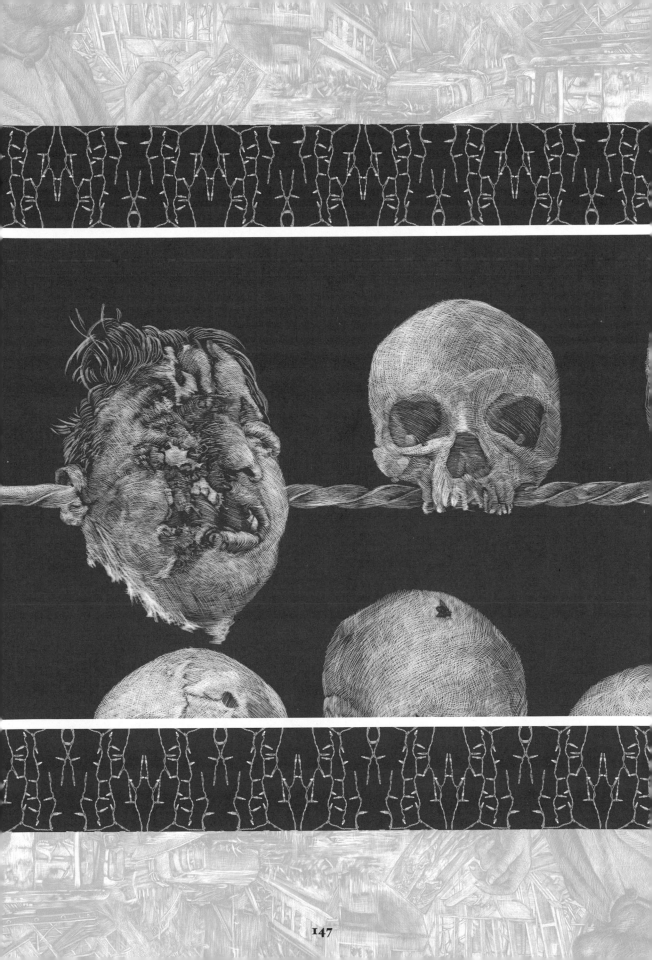

o matter when these words are stated they will be out of date, and yet current. The numbers will change, the dates turn over, the names come and then go. Phrases will be altered and new words will be used for old pains.

Still, it rolls on, the entire theater of dust and blood.

You want to know how it works? A man loses a load in an American city and now he must find the load or find money or he will die. So he looks into the matter and he sees a young couple, two lovers, talking to a Mexican he suspects, a man who is repairing their car. So he kidnaps the couple because he thinks they must be connected to the Mexican he suspects of taking his load and he tortures them and then he murders them and then he leaves their naked bodies under a bridge in this American city.

That is where a friend of mine comes in. He is a detective and he looks into the case and makes calls to people he knows in the drug world. He tells them this will cause you trouble and so they give him the name of the killer's supplier. And so he calls this supplier and says, if I can find your name and your phone number, I can find you and I will cause your business trouble.

The man says, the killer has fled to Mexico.

My friend says, he must be punished and until that happens then trouble is likely to come to your world and come often.

My friend knows what will happen. A phone call will be made to Mexico, someone will be told this man, this name, is causing problems for the business. And that this matter must be taken care of.

I don't know the rest because I know it. A body will be found on the edge of some Mexican town. There will be signs of torture and quite possibly mutilation—perhaps the genitals severed, or finger amputated and put in the mouth of the corpse. Most likely the body will show burn marks.

The problem will be solved. Justice will be done. Business will not be bothered in an American city for a spell.

Nothing will appear in the newspapers. But word will circulate to all the interested parties.

LALO'S SONG

Attorney: What will—what will happen to you if you are returned to—to Mexico?

Lalo: Well, they—they will kill me or they will torture me and then will kill me.

Attorney: Who will?

Lalo: Yeah, the police, the cartel, the government, it's all the same people.

Attorney: Why do you say it's the same people?

Lalo: Because the police works for the cartel.

Attorney: How do you know this?

Lalo: During the three years of working as a investigation [a U.S. government informant infiltrating the Vicente Carrillo Fuentes organization], I recorded and I showed that—that the police is under the order and to service the people from the cartel, inclusive this recordings were I would record the conversations that I would have with Santillán, and he would explain to me the arrangements that they would have with militaries with high executives, high-level government people.

Attorney: The—the arrangements that the cartel had with the military?

Lalo: They were militaries, with politics—politicians and with the police, that's for sure that they are under the orders.

Attorney: And when you say the police, are there many levels of police?

Lalo: Yes, there is three levels, federal, state, and municipal.

Attorney: Which ones are under the control of the cartel?

Lalo: All three of them.

Attorney: You indicated that you have recorded some conversations with Santillán where he explained arrangements that were made with the military and politicians. What—what specific arrangements did he tell you about politicians?

Lalo: No, that he didn't precisely, himself, well, the cartel had arrangements with people that were close to President Fox [of Mexico]. He explained to me that President Fox took—took the position to arrange, consult with the cartel from Juárez to—which it, which it means that he was going to attack the—the enemy cartels being from Tijuana and from the Gulf, and then the cartel from Juárez would be operating with this court, you know, without the government being—

Attorney: This is—

Lalo: —on—

Attorney: —what—

Lalo: —top of them.

Attorney: This is what Santillán told you?

Lalo: It's one of the conversations that we did have. Also, when I did go to Colombia to make arrangement with the Colombians, the plans was to come by sea, and the Mexico's navy, the ships, they're the ones that would get the drugs in the—in the sea—marina—ocean borders, you know, of the national territories. They, yeah, they kept close to what you call ground, firm ground, and the PGR then would fly this drugs to the—to Juárez, the city of Juárez.

Attorney: So from—from the—from the source of the drugs through the distribution, was all these arrangements made with different government parts?

Lalo: That's, yeah, that's the purpose to make arrangements with them so they won't have any losses. So they invite them, you know, to take part of the vehicle, and that way they avoid a war . . .

It is late in the day. The people who are serious about change are selling drugs and earning their broken nation tens of billions a year. The people who are serious about change are illegally migrating to the north and by this act increasing their income tenfold and by this act pumping well over twenty billion a year back into the nation they have fled.

We try to fit this into our notion of history and for centuries our notion of history has been progressive, that things get better, that an invisible hand guides us or invisible gods guide us, every generation lives better than the one before, and the way this is accomplished, the system, well, it will work anywhere if folks will just give it a chance and so, you see, the future is the past only nicer and nicer and there is no downbeat, just endless upticks and the markets vary but are certain, the energy arrives to satisfy our hungers, the food is bountiful, the women go to surgeons and come out the right size, and the poor will vanish, we have a plan, and war will vanish, we have right on our side, and drugs will vanish, we will live with material bliss and ignorance will vanish and violence will vanish and the sea will cough up its fishes

and loaves, and . . . we have the faith and will keep the faith and so there is nothing to worry about. And anything we worry about is really temporary because something will turn up and fix it.

Still, there is a small house on a calle in Juárez with a patio. And there are other houses in the city just like it. And in other cities. And these houses seem to be multiplying.

But here is where we stop and turn off the message machine and go back to the history that comforts us, that faith of our fathers.

alo continues to fight deportation to Mexico where he almost certainly will be murdered. Santillán is offered a deal by the U.S. government—take a twenty-five-year sentence and avoid a trial for murder. He accepts. By this plea bargain, the U.S. government avoids having Lalo ever take the stand and tell his tale. Or as Santillán's attorney put it, "Their star witness is a renegade, untrustworthy, a scam. I think the government didn't want him to take the stand."

Many agree that the government did not want Lalo on the stand, but not because he was a scam.

anet met Luis and they fell in love and married. And then one day Luis went to work.

My name is Janet Padilla.

I am over the age of twenty-one years and in all ways competent to make this affidavit.

All of the facts stated herein are within my personal knowledge and are true and correct.

I have been a legal resident of the United States since 1986 and I am eligible to become a citizen.

I was married to Luis Padilla in 1996 and remained very close to him during our marriage.

We have three children.

I spoke to my husband at least four or five times a day on his cell phone.

On or about January 14, 2004, my husband left the house in the morning but never made it to work at International Freight Line Service where he worked as a mechanic.

He did not answer his telephone.

I began to search for him.

Shortly thereafter, all his family members began to search.

That same day we found my husband's car with the keys in the ignition and the door open.

It appeared that the inside of the car had been thoroughly searched.

And, the gate to the property was left open.

It appeared that whoever left the property, left in a hurry.

I became extremely frightened for my husband's safety.

After that morning, I never saw my husband again.

I reported the disappearance to the local authorities.

Two weeks after his disappearance, the Mexican authorities in Juárez, Mexico, Antisecuestro [Anti-kidnapping] department called me to identify a body.

I found my husband.

Although his body had partially decomposed, there were obvious signs of abuse.

His hands and feet had been bound with duct tape.

His head and mouth were also partially bound with duct tape.

His pants were soaked in blood, especially in the groin area.

It appeared to me that Luís, my husband, had been tortured to death.

he man I kept meeting and talking with off the record finally decided to go on the record. His letter to the head of ICE in El Paso after the near-death experience of the DEA agents and their families in Juárez became public. So Sandalio González's anger poured into public view: ". . . Following the evacuation of our personnel . . . , ICE agents, with your concurrence, refused to immediately present the CS [confidential source] to Mexican Federal authorities so that his testimony could be used as probable cause necessary to arrest the corrupt police officials. . . . Now these dangerous killers are at large. To make matters worse, you would not allow the CS to call [Mexican police commander Miguel Loya Gallegos] so that Mexican Federal authorities could arrest him for his participation in the murders. . .

". . . This situation is so bizarre that even as I'm writing to you it is difficult for me to believe it. I have never before come across such callous behavior by fellow law enforcement officers. The bottom line is that as a result of these actions, [Loya] and other murder suspects are now fugitives. There

was no logical reason to prevent the CS from calling [Loya] so Mexican authorities could arrest him. . . . Santillán's] subsequent indictment for murders that occurred after August 5, that could have been prevented, is disturbing. . . ."

Yes. We all seem to try to keep believing, believing that the Mexican Federal authorities would do the right thing, that murderers would be arrested and tried, that murders could be prevented, that there is a system and that this system works. And of course there is a system, one that stood by in silence while twelve or fourteen or more people were murdered, one that cut deals with the head of the killers rather than have things heard in open court, one that supplied police for the killings, one that takes money so drugs may move, one that continues on today as if none of these things happened in those days gone by and those coming toward us.

I sip my coffee in the morning, my glass of wine in the evening, and the belief floods my body and I hear birds singing and the dead go silent and all is well again.

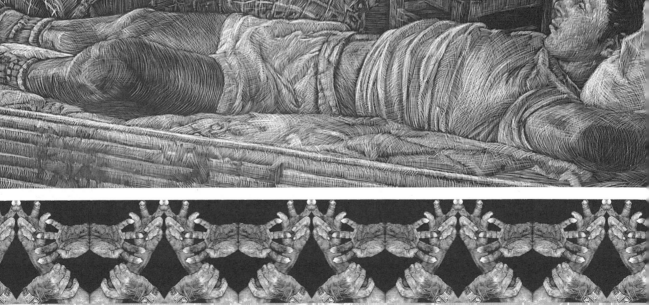

We can dismiss the dead because they were crooked or they were greedy, because they wanted easy money and fast women and gangster life. This helps get rid of them. But one thing always strikes me—they were dreamers. They see men and women and children die around them and yet they think they will live. They see deals go bad, the money vanish, and yet they think they will get rich. They see the duct tape seal the mouth, the cord strangle the throat, and all this happens because someone trusted someone and relaxed and thought things were okay, in fact that things were looking up. That is the fatal moment, the moment of ease and trust because once you arrive at that moment you are ripe for betrayal.

Just as Lalo is in the house with the killers and worried he might be betrayed and at

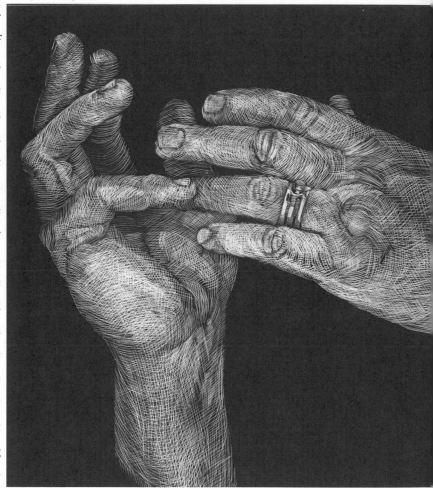

the same time, he is betraying his colleagues in the house to the U.S. government, and Santillán is routinely betraying people like  Fernando, his childhood friend, and Vicente Carrillo is ordering the murder of employees who serve him faithfully and ICE is listening, letting a known drug smuggler commit murders because he is making their cases and thereby their careers and that is their big dream coming out of the house of death, this notion of advancement and promotions and this same lust courses through the U.S. Attorney's office where the headline busts move right along down the line and it is very difficult to say what these U.S. federal people are betraying because, in the end, it is very hard to remember what they believe or could betray.

Dreams, everyone needs them, even the killers, even the greedy, even the betrayers, even those strangling in the appetites of career, even the corrupt, even the damned and the lost, even I need dreams as I write these words and I just came out of the grocery with a bag full of things, shrimp, andouille, celery, bell peppers, green onions, a yellow onion, parsley, two bottles of wine, going to make a gumbo, add cayenne, some tomato paste, a stock brewed out of the shrimp shells, going to have us a time, and when I was a boy a man gave a speech and said he had a dream about all kinds of people of different colors doing just fine and then after a while he was cut down and went to his grave and still I keep dreaming. In the parking lot of the supermarket a fat woman with bare arms walked toward me and her fleshy limbs danced with big tattoos and her short hair was dyed red with a wide blonde streak in front and her face could not smile but her body said dream, dream, dream and in the patio of the house of death they shoveled over dreamers, and sweating men stood over the graves and kept dreaming and it goes on and on because that is how we avoid this hard reality.

There is a time out of mind and in this space death comes and leaves little tiny prints on our souls.

Two bullets tear through his body one afternoon in Colonia Rancho Anapra as he exits this world at the corner of Moonfish and Hipocampo streets.

His car is found a few blocks away at the corner of Needlefish and Hammerfish.

He is about twenty and known as El Cholito, the Little Hoodlum.

He belongs to the Wonderlook gang in Juárez.

He dies near the wall that attempts to lock one nation out of another.

He dies almost beneath notice.

She is going to her wedding one afternoon in Juárez.

She finds a crying baby in a box out back of the church between barrels of garbage.

The baby girl is covered with excrement and blood and still has its umbilical cord.

The caretaker of the church is upset.

He asks what kind of mother would put a human being out by the barrels of garbage.

Besides, dogs look there for food.

The Mexican government has announced that jailed cartel leaders continue to run their businesses from jail.[3] Jose Luis Santiago Vasconcelos, Mexico's top drug prosecutor, explained, "The fight against drug trafficking doesn't end with detention. It's only the beginning. It's the beginning of a whole new battle." Three of the agents working with Lalo in the Juárez death-house matter may face criminal charges, according to U.S. officials. The two people in ICE who supervised these agents have been transferred from El Paso to Washington.[4] Seven months after the dead erupted from their graves in the Juárez death house, ICE brought Lalo and his girlfriend out of their haven in the United States for some unfinished business in El Paso. Before Lalo left town again, five people were dead, three of them residents of El Paso. Since then Lalo has disappeared back into his American sanctuary.

I am sitting having coffee with a reporter from Juárez, one who lives in El Paso. He notes that Lalo lived just down the street from him for a spell. In the U.S. press, the informant's name has been given as Jesús Contreras. The reporter says this is a false name and that his real name is Guillermo Eduardo Ramírez Peyro. I dutifully write this down.

It is like recording a mist.

The reporter leans forward and says softly, "Juárez is a very dangerous city."

Everything returns to scale. The dead fall silent again.

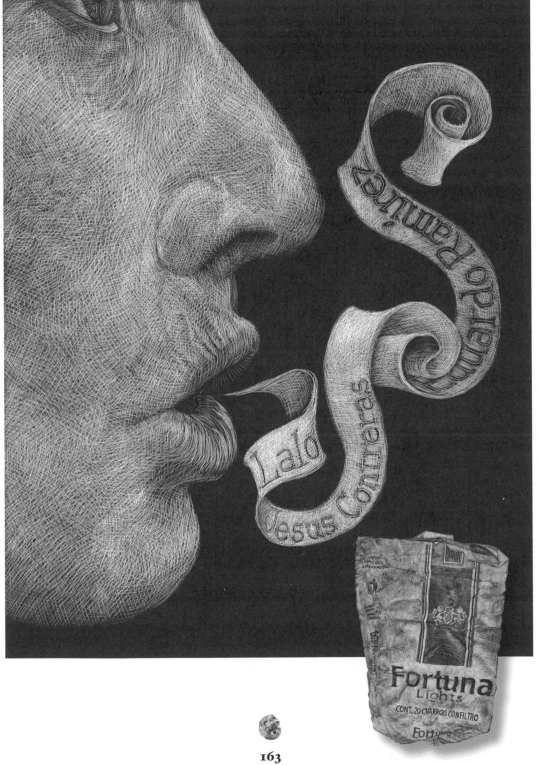

a note on this story

Anyone interested in learning more about the house of death should examine the reporting of Alfredo Corchado at the *Dallas Morning News* and the work done by Bill Conroy (www.narconews.com). The various interviews and depositions arranged here as "Lalo's Song" can be found on the Narconews site under "Bill Conroy House of Death." Lalo's comments have been silently elided to dispatch the lists of non-recurring names of accomplices he gives at times that would confuse the reader and to leave out other instances that add nothing to this story.

"It Ain't Necessarily So," by George Gershwin and Ira Gershwin, comes from *Porgy and Bess*, the great American opera about all that unfinished business that a business culture never seems to have the time or energy to fix.

Details about this case will probably emerge for years, just as eventually Lalo will either be returned to Mexico and promptly murdered, or released from U.S. custody and, should he wish, be able to speak more freely.

And more such houses will open, though we are not likely to learn much of them since it is doubtful any U.S. agency will broadcast a killing in the near future.

The pain can be too much and then we retreat from what has happened, we dismiss what we have learned and we fall back on what we once knew and now insist is still true. This is our modus operandi and it has served us well.

In the case of the house of death in Juárez, DEA reeled from the fact that two of its agents in Juárez and possibly their families could have been kidnapped, taken to the house on Parsioneros Street, murdered, and planted in the patio because of a rogue operation by a fellow U.S. agency on the line. So they created a timeline to make sense of what had happened and almost happened.

It is a useful document. For those who insist on order, it brings order. For those who deny the chaos and violence on the line, it insists on chaos and violence. Soon it will gather dust in some office file and be forgotten. Just as the dead are now barely remembered and the house of death is now just one more condominium in a middle-class neighborhood where roses bloom in yards and children have birthday parties.

http://narcosphere.narconews.com/userfiles/70/DEAtimeline.pdf

Notes

[1] *Frontera NorteSur,* January–February 2004, http://www.nmsu.edu/-frontera/.

[2] Lalo here and in other excerpts from the television interview is speaking in English and as a result his command of the language sometimes falters.

[3] Will Weissert, "Mexican Drug War Pits Cartel vs. Convicts," Associated Press, January 14, 2005.

[4] Alfredo Corchado, "U.S. Agents May Face Charges in Killing," *Dallas Morning News,* September 30, 2004.

ACKNOWLEDGMENTS

Charles Bowden's words convey what it is to move through Juárez—a dream and the Last Judgment rolled into one. And these words feed my drawings. Graphic designer Kelly Leslie skillfully orchestrated the visual and verbal dirge that is *Dreamland*. Our collaborative experiment has been time well spent.

A number of artist residencies and foundations directly supported my drawing habit during the development of this book. They include the Border Art Residency, El Paso Community Foundation, Jentel Foundation and Residency, and Larry E. Elsner Art Foundation. Over the years and throughout the creation of *Dreamland*, Kevin Avants, Sandy Besser, Terry Etherton, Michelle Ouellette, and Julie Sasse have supported my work with their thoughtfulness, encouragement, and friendship.

I am deeply grateful to the citizens of Ciudad Juárez, but most of all to Julián Cardona, who revealed to me the dark beauty of his city. I would also like to thank Hector Hawley, Chief of Forensics, Chihuahua State Police, and the staff of the Juárez morgue for their kindness in the midst of an epidemic of death.

Molly Molloy willingly shared photographs and insights about Ciudad Juárez and the *frontera*, not to mention her jovial companionship in all manner of wreckage. I thank John Dilg for teaching me how formidable marks can be. My drawings would never have otherwise existed. I am very grateful to the University of Texas Press editors and staff for their enthusiasm, guidance, and many hours of work on these pages. Also, *Dreamland* would not have been possible without the photographers who have documented my work during the past several years, including Piotr Chizinski, Tim Fuller, Wendy McEahern, Chas McGrath, and Rudy Torres.

Finally, I want to thank my parents, Edward and Virginia Brown; my children, Matthew Wagner and Elizabeth Wagner; and my husband, Peter, for all the rewards that family bestows . . . and for their willingness to serve as models. I apologize for not mentioning the names of each of the other many individuals to whom I am indebted for their kindness and contributions as I cut and scraped my way through *Dreamland*. You know who you are. I owe you big-time.

Alice Leora Briggs